The Game That Changed
Pro Football

The Game That Changed Pro Football

Stephen Hanks

A Birch Lane Press Book
Published by Carol Publishing Group

A Birch Lane Press Book
Published by Carol Publishing Group

Editorial Offices
600 Madison Avenue
New York, NY 10022

Sales & Distribution Offices
120 Enterprise Avenue
Secaucus, NJ 07094

In Canada: Musson Book Company
A division of General Publishing Co. Limited
Don Mills, Ontario

Manufactured in the United States of America
10 9 8 7 6 5 4 3 2 1

Library of Congress Cataloging-in-Publication Data

Hanks, Stephen.
        The game that changed pro football / Stephen Hanks.
              p.   cm.
        "A Birch Lane Press book."
        ISBN 1-55972-012-3 : $18.95
        1. New York Jets (Football team)--History. 2. Baltimore Colts
(Football team)--History. 3. Super Bowl Game (Football)--Case
studies. I. Title.
GV956.N42H36   1989
796.332'64'097471--dc20   89-22166
                                                    CIP

TO BEA FOR BELIEVING

Acknowledgments

Special thanks go to the following people who helped bring this book across the goal line before the final gun went off: To my publisher Steven Schragis, a fellow Jets fan who brought his passion to the project, my editor Sandy Richardson for his guidance, and my agent Joe Vallely for his encouragement and support; to Jim Morganthaler and Steve Bloom for invaluable help in research and interviewing; to Barry Hanks and Lorraine Sklerov for secretarial assistance; to Leonard Hanks for the Jets genes; to Berry Stainback for his advice and consul; to Paul Zimmerman for imparting his vast knowledge and saving his old Jets media guides; to Allen Barra for his unique football mind. Many thanks also to the National Football League Alumni Association, Steve Sabol of NFL Films, Wayne Lyttle of Namanco Productions, Doug Kelly of NBC Sports publicity, and, of course, the Super Bowl III Champions, the 1968 New York Jets, who made it all possible.

Contents

Introduction

There are hundreds of important games, moments, and records in American sports history, but there are few truly memorable scores. Pro football experts could probably recite the winner and the loser of all 23 Super Bowls, but only the most encyclopedic minds could remember the score of each contest. Except one.

16-7. It may well be pro football's most celebrated score since it represents a game that was both a great upset and a game that changed the way the nation thought about pro football. It was the score of the New York Jets victory over the Baltimore Colts in the 1969 Super Bowl III.

A generation has grown up since January 12, 1969, but just say "16-7" to a New York sports fan over 30 and he'll probably tell you where he was at the memorable moment when a supposedly overmatched team from an "inferior" league achieved something almost everyone said was impossible.

Few people who picked the Jets to win that day would have guessed that 1969 would be remembered for a football game as much as for the more "important" events of the year. Richard Nixon had just become the 36th President. Protests over the Vietnam War were raging throughout the country. Neil Armstrong became the first man to walk on the moon. The most famous rock concert ever was held in Woodstock, New York. (In fact, Max Yasgur, the owner of the farm which served as the concert site, was one of the many Jets fans at the Super Bowl that January.) The game between the anti-establishment Jets of the upstart, nine-year-old American Football League and the conservative Colts of the wealthy and powerful 49-year-old National Football League was in many ways a metaphor for the times.

But was it really a game that changed pro football?

Weeb Ewbank, whose coaching helped the Jets prevail 20 years ago, modestly downplays the game's impact. "They said the game I coached when the Colts won the [1958 NFL] championship in sudden death changed football forever. I thought they exaggerated then, too."

But Johnny Sample, who played on both championship teams, says: "The two games don't even compare. I know the 1958 game increased the popularity of football, but only a small number of people actually saw the game on television. There's not nearly as much written about the '58 game and most fans don't remember it now. They say it was the greatest game ever played, but I guarantee you, if you ask football fans to name six players from that game, they wouldn't be able to do it. Every football fan knows about Super Bowl III. Everybody knows who played in that game, what the circumstances were when it was played, what the score was, and why it was such a big deal when we [the Jets] won it."

One misconception about the game is that the Jets victory prompted the merger of the AFL and the NFL. In reality, there would never have been a Super Bowl had not the rival leagues already agreed to join forces in 1966, following a bitter competition for talent (including scouts from one league "kidnapping" players to keep the other league from signing them). It was a war which escalated in 1965 when Alabama quarterback Joe Namath was signed by the AFL's New York franchise (who outbid the NFL's St. Louis Cardinals) for the then-unprecedented sum of $427,000. Club owners in both leagues soon realized that a merger was imperative if they were to keep player salaries down and profits up. (The 1966 merger agreement became official on February 1, 1970, and that year, the leagues played as two separate conferences under the NFL banner.)

Another fallacy is that Super Bowl III was a well-played edge-of-the-seater. Like many Super Bowls that would follow, it was not a very exciting affair, only one touchdown being scored in the first half. The Jets executed a rather conservative but brilliant run-oriented game plan, whereas the Colts blundered at nearly every critical moment. What made the game a thriller was the sense during the third quarter that the underdog AFL representative might actually *win*. It was at that point the game took on an aura of wonder and excitement. Everyone realized that the younger league would finally have to be perceived as the established league's equal. When it was over, the AFL and NFL had become one, spiritually, as well as contractually, and the "Super Bowl"—which hadn't been so named until the Jets-Colts clash—promptly became the biggest sporting event in America, often treated with a reverence usually reserved for religious holidays.

Like that 1958 Baltimore Colts-New York Giants championship game, the Jets' victory was pivotal in generating intense fan interest in pro football. Super Bowl III was the sport's "Big Bang," creating a vast new world of stars, fans, television contracts and money. Television audiences on "Super Sunday" grew from approximately 20 million viewers for Super Bowl III to 102 million in 1978 for Super Bowl XII, at that time the largest audience for any show in television history. "Super Bowl parties" became a national tradition, along with ABC-TV's "Monday Night Football" with Howard Cosell, which began broadcasting 13 games a season starting in 1970. In the same year, the two other major networks—CBS and NBC—signed new four-year contracts with the recently-merged NFL. Pro football was pronounced "The Game of the '70s," and according to a Louis Harris Sports Survey conducted in 1978, football had displaced baseball as the country's national pastime.

But two decades later, it is the romantic symbolism of the Super Bowl III story that still thrives like a classic fantasy tale and for his role in making the Jets' storybook victory one that has transcended sports, Joe Namath has become as immortal as any hero in mythology.

In Namath's case, the facts helped create the legend. The AFL had lost the first two Super Bowls. The Colts had produced a 14-1 season and a 34-0 victory in the NFL Championship Game, and possessed what many called "the best defense in football history." Odds-makers like Jimmy "the Greek" Snyder had annointed the Colts 17 to 19-and-a-half-point favorites making the Jets one of the greatest underdogs in sports history. So when Namath boldly laughed in the face of these facts and made his famous guarantee" of victory, he became a legend the instant he followed through on that provocative promise.

By 1968, Namath had also become something of an underground hero to thousands of New York-area kids. Boys mimicked his quarterbacking mannerisms in touch football games and girls reacted to the charismatic quarterback with the Fu Manchu mustache as if he were a rock star. During this era of the "generation gap," most parents perceived Namath (in large part due to media characterizations) as an anti-hero, an arrogant skirt-chaser making too much money and with too flamboyant a lifestyle to be taken seriously as an athlete, let alone as a role model. Naturally, Namath's image among these particular fans received a face-lift when he became a champion.

Until that day, it wasn't easy wearing green and white in New York. The "big blue" of the NFL's New York Giants was still the preferred color of the city's football faithful. Those bold enough to don Jets jerseys often suffered taunts and ridicule. In tougher neighborhoods (like mine in the Bronx), the younger keepers of the NFL flame were not above using physical violence to express their superiority.

Minority Jets fans were made up of a reasonably large Long Island contingent and small pockets of enthusiasts sprinkled in the five boroughs. Jets fans were very distinct groups: people who couldn't acquire seasons tickets to Giants games at Yankee

Stadium; rebellious teenagers who found yet another political metaphor in rooting against the establishment Giants (their parents' team); enlightened adults (like my father) who, understanding there was enough good football talent coming out of the colleges, were willing to give the new league a chance to prove itself; young kids influenced by their father's interest in the Jets; and anybody who had not succumbed to the NFL's propaganda about its dominance.

But if Jets fans experienced an inferiority complex, it disappeared during three glorious hours on that January afternoon in 1969. With victory came an outpouring of pride; it was suddenly cool to be a Jets fan. Everybody bought a copy of the New York *Daily News*-sponsored 1968 highlights record album "Super Jets" and played it time and again. We could listen over and over again to Jets radio announcer Merle Harmon's Super Bowl III play-by-play as if it were simple but exquisite poetry. "Snell at the five, Snell at the three, Snell—touchdown! The Jets draw first blood!"

Twenty years later, I had the opportunity to experience those thrills again by reminiscing with the central characters of pro football's most famous Super Bowl game, athletes who were once my heroes and the heroes of part of New York. Though Super Bowl III may be one of the most rehashed events in sport's history, not one Jets player from that team seems to tire of retelling the stories that have become part of our sports lore. As the Jets' Hall of Fame wide receiver Don Maynard put it: "How could you ever get tired of talking about the greatest moment of your life, the thing you worked your whole career to achieve?"

Like many of the players, linebacker Larry Grantham's perspective on what the game meant to him has changed little in the 20 years since it was played. "At the time, I was just happy we had won the biggest football game in any one year," he relates. "But the older I get, the more important it becomes to me. We didn't realize at the time the impact that the game was going to have on pro football. I think had the NFL won that particular ball game like they had the other two Super Bowls, then the history of pro football in the United States might not be what it is today."

And when tight end Pete Lammons was asked if just playing in the legendary game made him feel immortal, he remarked in an exaggerated Texas drawl, "Well, hell, Steve, if we don't win that dang football game, you ain't talkin' to me right now."

This "oral history" of Super Bowl III and the New York Jets' incredible 1968 season is told from the point of view of the men who made it happen (with an occasional observation or opinion from members of the Colts to lend the losers perspective to the chapters on the famous game). Current interviews with nearly two dozen players, coaches, team officials, writers, and broadcasters closely associated with the team and the game are interspersed with notes, quotes and anecdotes from newspaper articles and books written 20 years ago (material from Dave Anderson's *Countdown to Super Bowl*, Lou Sahadi's *The Long Pass*, and Joe Namath's autobiography *I Can't Wait Until Tomorrow, 'Cause I Get Better Looking Every Day*, written with Dick Schaap, is sprinkled throughout). This is another telling of the legend; a celebration of a team and a season and a game that no true football fan, especially no New York football fan, will ever forget.

—Stephen Hanks

The Game That Changed
Pro Football

CHAPTER ONE

The Team: Characters With a Lot of Character

When the American Football League was born in 1960, its New York franchise was purchased by Harry Wismer, a sports broadcaster and promoter with limited financial resources. Three years and many bounced checks later, the team was sold to a syndicate headed by Sonny Werblin, an entertainment impresario with deep pockets. The transaction was the dawn of the struggling AFL. With a secure franchise in New York owned by a smart media man (Werblin, like Wismer before him, was instrumental in securing a network television contract for the new league), equality with the monolithic National Football League couldn't be very far away.

After Wismer's "Titans" (so named because, as Wismer said, "They're bigger than Giants") became Werblin's "Jets" (because it rhymed with "Mets") in March of 1963, the new owner's first major move was to hire Weeb Ewbank as coach. Small, rotund, and white-haired, Ewbank looked more like the Pillsbury doughboy's grandfather than a football coach who'd won two successive championships with the Baltimore Colts in 1958 and '59. Fired by the Colts and replaced by Don Shula following a 7-7 season in 1962, Ewbank was also appointed general manager under Werblin. With Sonny's bank account and Weeb's game-plans, the Jets promptly set out to do what Ewbank had accomplished at Baltimore—transform the team from a loser to a champion in just five years.

After four losing seasons, the Jets fell short of Ewbank's goal when in 1967 they lost three straight second-half games, finishing the year at 8-5-1, second to the Houston Oilers for the AFL's Eastern Division title. But a final-game 42-31 victory over San Diego and quarterback Joe Namath's pro record-setting 4,007 yards passing for the season gave the team and the coach reason to be optimistic about 1968.

The 1968 Jets were a fascinating melange of players; a few original Titans, free-agents who had been cut by NFL teams, high draft choices signed during the AFL-NFL bidding wars before the common draft began in 1967, and players acquired through trades with AFL teams. The sole high-priced star was at quarterback. Joe Namath had been signed by Werblin in 1965 for the unprecedented sum of $427,000. He was proving to be worth every penny, both for the Jets and the increasingly prosperous AFL. (Werblin, however, wouldn't be part of the Jets' success in 1968. He sold out to his partners before the season began.)

The defense, coached by assistants Walt Michaels and Buddy Ryan (both ultimately became head coaches), was relatively small in the lines, but it made up in speed and savvy for what it lacked in size. The one behemoth in the defensive line was the appropriately named Verlon Biggs, a 6'4", 265-pound end and two-time All-Star. Along side him on the front four was the extremely quick 6'5", 245-pound, second-year right tackle John Elliott. On the left side were the tackle-sharers platoon of Paul Rochester and Carl McAdams, and 6'2", 245-pound left end Gerry Philbin, on the verge of All-Pro status going into his fifth season.

The average size of the Jets' linebacking corps was 6'2", 225-pounds, numbers which in today's NFL would elicit yawns from the scouts. But modeled in the image of Michaels, a former Cleveland Browns linebacker, the Jets' threesome was as tough and as solid as any unit in the league. Cagey nine-year veteran and original Titan, Larry Grantham, soft-spoken but hard-tackling Al Atkinson, and mistake-free Ralph Baker played like assistant coaches on the field.

The secondary was a player personnel director's delight—all four had been signed as free agents. At cornerback, the Jets teamed young, fast Randy Beverly on the right side with the former Baltimore Colts veteran Johnny Sample on the left. Another ex-Colt, Bill Baird, was the free safety, while tough, quick Jim Hudson provided big-play potential at the strong safety spot. Cornell Gordon was an all-purpose backup in the secondary.

In punter Curley Johnson and field-goal specialist Jim Turner, the Jets had one of the AFL's best kicking games. Johnson, another original Titan, was a 12-year veteran with a career punting average of over 42 yards. He also played backup tight end and was the clubhouse clown. Turner, the third string quarterback, had led the Jets in scoring every season since joining the team as a free agent in 1964.

Two significant pre-season Ewbank trades bolstered both the kicking game and the protection for Joe Namath. In July, the general manager sent young backup quarterback Mike Taliafero to the Boston Patriots for veteran quarterback Babe Parilli. Besides providing experienced leadership behind Namath, the 14-year veteran would also become the holder for Jim Turner (making a major contribution to what became Turner's record-setting season). In August, Ewbank sent a third-round draft pick to the Houston Oilers for offensive guard Bob Talamini, a 10-year veteran and six-time All-AFL guard. Talamini would provide insurance just in case second-year left guard Randy Rasmussen or rookie right tackle Sam Walton faltered.

There was little chance of a breakdown at the left tackle or right guard positions, which were manned by 6'4", 280-pound All-Star Winston Hill and 6'1", 255-pound Dave Herman, respectively. At center was five-year man John Schmitt, who'd spent two years on the taxi squad before becoming a starter in 1966. Coached by Joe Spencer, the Jets' offensive line was the key unit on the team since it was responsible for protecting the man with the most expensive pair of knees in pro football, Joe Namath.

Besides setting a passing yardage record in '67, the often erratic Namath threw 26 touchdown passes, yet he also had a league-leading 28 interceptions, and was co-MVP of the league All-Star Game. The Jets surrounded Namath with explosive impact players. In the backfield were fullback Matt Snell and halfback Emerson Boozer, who were both coming off injury-plagued seasons. Snell, the 1964 Rookie of the Year, had torn knee cartilage in the '67 opener and missed seven games. Boozer had been brilliant early in his sophomore season, and with 10 touchdowns in seven games was rushing towards a slew of scoring records. But torn knee ligaments suffered in the season's eighth game had shelved him for the year. Both backs were superb blockers who could help protect Namath and the Jets needed them healthy in '68. If either failed to rebound, able veterans Bill Mathis, an original Titan, and Billy Joe, who had rushed for almost 2,000 career yards in five AFL seasons, provided backfield depth.

Among Namath's passing targets were arguably the best trio of receivers in the AFL, if not in all of pro football. Original Titan Don Maynard was an 11-year veteran, but still a burner at flanker, and was coming off a career-high 1,434 yards receiving season in '67. George Sauer Jr. (his father had been the Jets' player personnel director) was a sure-handed split end with deceptive moves. And sophomore Pete Lammons was a tough-blocking, tackle-breaking, 6'3", 228-pound tight end. Seven-year veteran Bake Turner, the Jets' Most Valuable Player in 1963 with over 1,000 yards receiving, was the team's number one pass-catcher off the bench. Offensive coordinator Clive Rush had molded this group into the AFL's number one passing offense in 1967.

Maynard, Sauer, Lammons and Turner had one other thing in common—they had all played college football in Texas and made their homes in the state. In fact, the unique camaraderie of the 1968 Jets stemmed in large part from the squad's deep Southern roots. Nine players went to Texas colleges and six others

4

graduated from Southern schools (Sauer, Lammons and Jim Hudson were all members of the Texas team that had beaten Joe Namath and Alabama in the 1956 Orange Bowl). They were all no doubt looking forward to visiting the south and the Orange Bowl again for a very big game sometime in January.

The Days of the Bounced Checks

LARRY GRANTHAM (LINEBACKER): In 1960, I was drafted by the Baltimore Colts of the NFL and the New York Titans of the new AFL. Weeb Ewbank was still the coach of the Colts and he told me that only three of the 30 or so rookies they had in camp were going to make their team, and that the odds of my making it were about 10 to one. Since the Titans were offering me the same money as Baltimore, I'd figure I'd take a chance and go to the new league. I knew I'd have a chance to play immediately and could find out whether I could hack it or not. In the back of my mind, I felt that if I proved myself and the new league folded, I could always go shopping for a job in the NFL.

By 1962, I was becoming an All-Pro, but the team was having a lot of financial problems. A bunch of us lived in the Concourse Plaza Hotel near Yankee Stadium and we were doing business with a bank right down the street. I was always interested in banking and got familiar with the bankers there. They used to laugh when we walked in to deposit our checks. They'd tell us we'd have to wait until they cleared because by then word had gotten out that the team was in financial trouble. So we'd have to get some money from other sources—friends, our families back home—just to live day to day. We tried not to let it distract us. We were all pretty naïve then and continued to take one day at a time figuring everything would work out.

Soon it got to the point where the checks wouldn't clear at all. At the beginning of the season, our paychecks bounced and the team didn't have the money for us to travel to Buffalo for our first game that season. We didn't work out all week, then the coaches helped us pay our way upstate for the game. Believe it or not, we won a ballgame that weekend.

5

We finally called the league office and [Kansas City Chiefs owner and a league founder] Lamar Hunt came in and paid everybody's back wages and saved us from disbanding. You know, up until that moment when we had to face the reality of the situation, we were still living in that fantasy world where everything would be fine and Wismer would find the money to pay us.

DON MAYNARD (WIDE RECEIVER): One of the biggest disappointments of those early years was that the New York fans never accepted us. I mean, we didn't expect people to break down the doors, but at most games you could almost count the fans in the stands on your fingers. They were the smallest crowds I'd ever played in front of. [In 1962, playing at the Polo Grounds, the team averaged just over 5,000 fans per game.] Even worse, the sportswriters often scoffed at us. The Giants had New York all to themselves then and we were treated like intruders and clowns.

DR. JAMES A. NICHOLAS (JETS' TEAM PHYSICIAN SINCE 1960): I may not have been a player, but I hated the Giants and was as much a bitter enemy of the NFL as any player. Guys like Grantham and Maynard used to park their cars outside the Polo Grounds and after a game they'd find their tires were slashed. And everybody would blame the Giants, even though they were across the river at Yankee Stadium. Harry Wismer sent a telegram to Washington, D.C., asking that the Giants be investigated for slashing the tires.

The New Beginning

MAYNARD: After Sonny Werblin and his group bought the team in '63, the atmosphere was more professional almost immediately, but there was a lot of friction in that first Jets training camp. Every day, a couple of old Titans were cut from the squad and one or two ex-Colts would come into camp. All the ex-Colts stuck together, the ex-Titans stuck together, the new players who came in as free agents stuck together. We ex-Titans kinda felt like the underdogs since the front office seemed to want a new image and wanted to get rid of any references to the Titans.

But everything turned out great that first Jet season. More people came out to see us play and the players felt secure knowing the new owners had some money behind them. When we moved over to the new Shea Stadium in '64, it was like another world—new locker rooms and everything. And the fans finally started to come out to see us play. We must have had more fans that first year at Shea than all the years at the Polo Grounds put together. I didn't feel like an orphan any more.

GRANTHAM: You know, we went through the first few years never signing a number one or number two draft choice, or anybody who really could play football. Then we get Matt Snell and Gerry Philbin in '64 and Joe Namath in '65 and you see that things are being done to upgrade the ball club and that the goal was winning.

JOE NAMATH (QUARTERBACK): When I was making my decision about signing with the Jets, I couldn't avoid being concerned about the AFL's "inferiority" and whether the league really had a future. After all, that's all the media talked about then. But I got some great advice from Coach [Bear] Bryant [at Alabama], who always influenced me to keep an open mind about the AFL and the Jets' proposals. I realized I would have an opportunity to go from one of the greatest and grandest teachers of young men in Bear Bryant to Weeb Ewbank, who had proven he could win in the big leagues and who had coached one of the all-time great quarterbacks in Johnny Unitas. The prospect of working with Weeb Ewbank and Mr. Werblin, who made the whole operation seem major league, really won me over. It wasn't the need to get involved in the rivalry between the two leagues or even necessarily wanting to play in New York. But I soon learned the importance of New York for a sportsman and what opportunities could be afforded to you in New York if you were successful. Had I known all that beforehand, I probably would have signed with the Jets earlier. But I was too naïve at that time to understand all that.

JOHNNY SAMPLE (CORNERBACK): When I got to camp after joining the team in '66, I saw these defensive guys running around and I said, "Sheet, I don't know what I'm doing here. These guys can't play." So Weeb called me in one day and said, "Look, we can win the championship and get to the Super Bowl game. All you have to do is lead the defense. We're building a great offense behind Joe. If you can get the secondary together, we can win this thing." I said, "Weeb, no way these guys are going to the Super Bowl, they look horrible." He said, "Yeah, I know, but they've got some ability and all we need to do is play together as a team and we can do it." Damn if Weeb didn't turn out to be right.

SONNY WERBLIN (OWNER 1963-1967): When we were rebuilding in 1963, I remember Weeb saying that defense was the name of the game. He said, "Let's draft athletes, no matter what position they played in college." That's how we built the defense. Jim Hudson was a quarterback at Texas and he became a safetyman for us. Ralph Baker was an offensive end at Penn State, and he became our corner linebacker. We were even thinking of playing our fullback Matt Snell at linebacker, because we had no one else, but Woody Hayes [Snell's coach at Ohio State] talked us out of it.

PAUL ZIMMERMAN (*SPORTS ILLUSTRATED* football writer who covered the Jets for the *New York Post* in '60s and '70s): Ewbank built the Jets from a garbage franchise into a Super Bowl champion through his choice of free agents. He had made friends in his NFL days, and people didn't mind passing along tips to Weeb. It's kind of ironic now, but Winston Hill, Bill Baird, Bake Turner and Mark Smolinski were all guys cut by the Colts that Don Shula suggested contact the Jets. The whole Super Bowl defensive backfield—Sample, Beverly, Baird and Hudson— were free agents. Al Atkinson had been cast off by Buffalo and

John Schmitt and Jim Turner couldn't make it with the then lowly Washington Redskins.

Weeb Ewbank—Head Coach

CURLEY JOHNSON (PUNTER): I broke in with Weeb at Baltimore in 1958. I spent the year on the taxi squad and Weeb wanted me to hang around in case of an emergency or something. I didn't want any part of that shit, so I went and played in Canada in '59. When I heard the AFL was gonna put a team in Dallas [the Texans, the team which became the Kansas City Chiefs], which was my home town, I signed with them. I got traded to the Titans in '61. When I read during the '63 off-season that Weeb had become the coach of the Jets, I figured, well, if there's any bitterness I'd be the first sonofabitch he runs off. But Weeb's forte was picking up good players who would be hungry and play hard for him for very little money. Most of our team was filled with a bunch of castoffs. But Weeb gave guys an opportunity to make it and so we worked harder to prove ourselves.

MAYNARD: Weeb was great in the way he handled ballplayers and situations. We'd never work out over an hour and 45 minutes because he didn't want us to leave our game on the practice field. Now that philosophy right there needs to be put up in big capital letters for some of these head coaches today. Some of them think that when it ain't goin' right, well, they'll make it go right by overworking people, but that ain't the way it goes. And Weeb had everything so organized that you never left your mental deal in the meetings. And, you know, the year we won the Super Bowl, I would say there was only one of seven home games where we worked out on a Saturday. We were always fresh as could be come Sunday.

NAMATH: The thing that struck me about Weeb initially was the tremendous difference between his personality and Coach Bryant's. I'll never forget my first professional game, an exhibition against the Houston Oilers in Alexandria, Virginia. I was standing on the sidelines next to Weeb when Don Maynard missed catching a pass. Right away Weeb sends in a substitute and says, "Shoot, Don, what kind of effort is that?" Don looked at Weeb just as calm and cool as could be and said, "Weeb, what do you want for $50 a game?" And I almost fell down. I couldn't believe I heard a player talk to a coach that way. I was in shock because at Alabama I played for a coach who was a very firm disciplinarian. But the older, more mature and more intelligent I got, the more Weeb changed in my eyes. I realized that the best move Mr. Werblin and the other owners made was bringing in Weeb Ewbank. He had a tremendous ability for recognizing talent. His organizational efforts in putting together that Jets team have never been given enough credit.

In his dealing with me during my first year, Weeb didn't push me when everybody else, including myself, wanted me in there at quarterback. Weeb knew there were a lot of things I had to learn and absorb and he didn't want all that thrown at me right away.

ZIMMERMANN: Weeb was hot shit. In '67, he put in this cockamamie offense for a game against the Houston Oilers where he had no backs in the backfield. Both backs were flanked outside and the wide receivers were in tight. So you had four wide outs, a tight end and no backs. And though he was practicing it—they actually used it in the first series of downs and got a touchdown out of it—the rule was that if he was putting in anything new, you couldn't write about it. And he never barred anybody from his practice, you know, visiting writers, he didn't care. Anybody could come to practice. And so I'm watching this shit and afterwards I say, "Weeb, if I'm a Houston writer and I see this and I come over to you after practice and ask you about it, what are you gonna tell me?" And he says, "I would tell you I'm getting my defense ready for that crazy shit the Oilers use."

MAYNARD: I think the greatest move Weeb made at the beginning of the '68 season was moving our training camp from Peekskill to Hofstra University, which was in Hempstead, Long Island. We'd been in Peekskill because Sonny's [Werblin's] son was going to the school, but when we moved, boy, were we happy. Instead of moaning and griping every night about the food, the showers, and the rooms, we all began talkin' about football. We began to enjoy training camp because we had a nice place to eat, air-conditioned dorms and a good practice field. I'm sure it had a lot to do with our winning the championship, because the change brought the guys together more.

Weeb came a long way that year in his relationship with the players. With Sonny gone, the new owners gave him a free rein and he didn't have to worry about interference. He ran the team the way he wanted to run it and got rid of the players that I felt prevented us from going to the Super Bowl in '67.

To me personally, though, Weeb was three different people. As a coach, I liked him about 90 percent of the time. As a man, away from football, I truly loved him. But as a general manager to argue with about salary, I hated him. I'd tell him, "Weeb, you're so tight, you'd steal from your own mother."

JIM HUDSON (SAFETY): It was really fun negotiating with Weeb. After their rookie year, very few guys signed before we got to training camp. Hell, that would give you a reason to argue with Weeb and then if you got tired of training camp, you could walk out, blame it on a contract squabble and go play around in the city. Basically, all of us knew that whatever Weeb told us he was gonna pay never varied less than five hundred to a thousand from what you wanted, but everybody argued with him because it was so much fun.

But Weeb was a very unique guy. You could be up there at one in the afternoon just screamin' and cussin' and fightin' about your contract, then later on the practice field he'd walk up to you say, "Hey, Jim, how you doing?" like he hadn't seen me in a month, like nothin' had ever happened."

RALPH BAKER (LINEBACKER): In everything Weeb did the dollar was instrumental. He would delay a flight so we could eat on the plane and he wouldn't have to pay us per diem for one more meal. But Weeb could coach in any atmosphere; he could be successful today. Most coaches wouldn't allow guys to drink in the hotel bar, but Weeb took just the opposite stand. He knew guys were gonna drink so he wanted you to drink in the hotel bar. He'd even come in and buy you a drink so he could keep an eye on you. He knew who'd had one too many and would tell somebody, "Hey, your roommate over there is pushing the limit. Why don't you get him out of here." I thought a lot of things Weeb did were way ahead of his time."

MATT SNELL (FULLBACK): My rookie year [1964] I got $20,000 with a $30,000 signing bonus, then went out and led the team in rushing and receiving, won the Rookie of the Year award and made the AFL All-Star Game. I was in the Naval Reserve until training camp the next year so I didn't negotiate my new contract until I met with Weeb in May. He said, "We appreciate the year you gave us and Sonny's authorized me to offer you a raise in appreciation." I said, "Fine, what is it?" They said "$2,500." I said, "Give me a break. If I hadn't started, you probably would have cut my salary. If you don't have better numbers than that, I'll see you in training camp." About a week or two later, I met with Sonny and he said, "We thought we made you a fair offer." I said, "You've got to be kidding me. You think $2,500 is fair?" I ended up getting $25,000 from Sonny and I'm still not sure whether Weeb was authorized to offer me that much or not. But I wouldn't be surprised if he was. It was bad news having the head coach as the general manager.

As far as being a motivator, Weeb didn't give these tremendous pep talks. His feeling was that you're a professional being paid to do a job and if he had to give a motivational speech every week, he'd better start looking for other players. He believed you should motivate yourself.

JIM TURNER (PLACE KICKER): To tell you the truth, Weeb and I never got along because he was also the general manager. But as a kicker, I liked his philosophy. I'd played with some coaches who would always be upset at settling for three points. Well, that's stupidity in coaching. Weeb knew from his experience with Paul Brown and Lou Groza [Ewbank had been an assistant coach for the Cleveland Browns in the early '50s] that a solid kicking game could win you a championship. And in 1968, he was right.

I don't think Weeb's been given enough credit. I mean he won the Super Bowl and it did it with only four assistant coaches. Now, these teams have a fleet of coaches and they all get in each other's way. I mean the nonsense we see today. The Denver Broncos have about 16 coaches.

SNELL: I can't say that much about Weeb as a coach because he didn't do a lot of coaching. Being both coach and general manager, he was very good at delegating authority. And he had very good people under him. Chuck Knox [offensive line coach in the mid-'60s], Clive Rush, Walt Michaels and Buddy Ryan all became head coaches. Weeb did the coaching on Sunday, but left the rest up to the assistants.

Don Maynard—Flanker

MAYNARD: My first year as a pro was 1958 with the New York Giants after playing for Texas Western for three years. I spent the season returning kicks and playing wide receiver. In fact, I returned the opening kickoff in the game they called "the greatest ever" between the Colts and the Giants. But my Giant career ended during a practice the next season. Frank Gifford was playing quarterback and since I was the number one left halfback behind Gifford, I was running some sweeps. Well, I run the play the right way, I mean I knew the plays, and [coach] Allie Sherman says, "Let's run the play over. And get to running, Maynard." So, naturally, I didn't know I wasn't runnin', so I tried to run even harder. And Sherman says, "Let's run it again." He says, "This ain't track, you're playing football. Your strides are too long." I said, "I can cover more ground in one step than anybody you got out here does in three." It was probably the first time I ever talked back to a coach. He just exploded and sent me down to the other end of the field to stand by the goal

13

posts. He ended up cutting me and kept an ole boy named Joe Biscaha. Heck, I could run faster backwards than he could run frontwards.

I'm not trying to brag a little bit, but I could play halfback, receiver, defensive safety, run back kicks. I was probably as good an all-around back as there was on that Giants team except maybe for Gifford and I was a lot faster than he was.

The next year, I played in Canada, mostly at safety. A lot of people didn't know this, but Vince Lombardi, who'd been a Giants assistant coach, had picked up my NFL option and wanted to know if I was interested in playing for the Green Bay Packers. I told him I was getting to play offense and defense and I loved to play defense. He asked me if I was happy there and I told him yes and that was the end of it. See, I had a pretty good idea the AFL was gonna be formed the next year, so when I signed my Canadian League contract in '59, I didn't sign with an option year. I wound up being one of the first New York Titans that was signed.

Nine years later, I passed Raymond Berry for the total yards receiving record [9,435]. There were some comments here and there that my record was tainted because I broke it playing in the AFL, but I didn't pay much attention to it. Nothing ever really bothered me except taxes. I just knew that each yard had come hard and, naturally, I was tickled with the record. The one I really wanted was to become the first receiver to get 10,000 yards. To me that was like runnin' the first four-minute mile. [In his career, Maynard caught 633 passes for 11,834 yards.]

Aside from that, I really wasn't aware of records. You know, I sat out the last game of the regular season in '68 with a pulled left hamstring even though I knew the season-yardage leadership was on the line. We'd already had the division won so it didn't make sense to chance tearing it and missing the championship game with the Raiders completely. Bake Turner replaced me and on the first play of the game we ran a flea-flicker and Joe threw one to Bake for something like 70 yards [71]. Bake got over 150 yards that game and got his first game ball. On the flight back to New York, Bake was treating that ball like a baby in his arms. He was saying, "You ever smell a football? Nothing sweeter than the smell of leather." Anyway, I probably would have gotten as many yards as Bake had I played. It cost me leading the league in total yardage by 15 behind Lance Alworth [of the San Diego Chargers]. But like I tell people, "I traded those 15 yards for the 15 thousand we got for winning the Super Bowl."

SNELL: I'll tell you the honest truth. Know what made Maynard great? George Sauer. Maynard wasn't a workaholic and never knew how to run patterns. But he saw Sauer and Namath working together on pass routes after practice. He started working with them and finally learned how to control that tremendous speed. He also learned how to fight for the ball, to dive for it. When I first came to the Jets, Maynard's uniform was almost as clean at the end of the game as it was in the beginning. If the ball was thrown right to him, he'd catch it. But dive, forget about it. Later on his career, he'd make that catch, like the ones he made in the title game against the Raiders in '68.

GRANTHAM: The main problem Weeb always had with Don was the fact that Don wouldn't block on running plays. See, in the Titans' first year, Don was leading the league with about 70 catches with two or three games left. We're out in Denver and Don threw a critical block on a screen pass to break an 80-yard run and he separated his shoulder. And to top it off, the play was called back because the receiver on the other side of the line was in motion. And so Don made up his mind that he was a pass receiver from then on. On a running play, he'd take his corner-back 20 to 30 yards deep, but Weeb didn't classify that as a block. It became one of those issues Weeb and Don could never settle, but Don was such a great pass receiver that he had to play.

Don and I were the closest of the close. He was probably the most eccentric guy I've ever been around. For example, his attitude about money. When I got to know him well, I started to question his finances when we'd go through a 10-cent toll booth and he'd want a receipt for his income taxes. When the team was still the Titans and we were worried about our checks clearing, Maynard would be the first guy at the bank trying to cash his check. That sucker could outrun us and beat us there all the time.

Then there was that time in Oakland, I think in '66, when one of the guys suggested somebody should jump in the hotel pool. Don said, "Put up some money and I'll do it." Another guy said, "Okay, but you've gotta jump off the board with your clothes on." We let him take off his cowboy boots, but he had to wear everything else including his green Jet blazer. We got a little over 50 bucks together and he dove in. One of the guys said, "Put up enough money and ol' Maynard would swim the Atlantic."

Don also owned his own uniform. He wanted his own shirt, his own pants. He owned his shoulder pads, helmet and shoes. He carried them home with him during the off-season. He didn't think he could feel the same way from what the team's equipment people gave him so he just kept his own.

JOHN ELLIOTT (DEFENSIVE TACKLE): I don't know who was tighter with the dollar, Ewbank or Don Maynard. One year they were negotiating a contract and they got it settled two or three days before the season started. Weeb told Don, "Don't tell anybody what you're making, I don't want that to get out." Maynard answered, "I won't Weeb, I'm just as ashamed of it as you are."

JIMMY ORR (BALTIMORE COLTS' RECEIVER): Don and I were roommates at the Blue-Gray All-Star game in 1958. He was a good guy, but you know what I remember most about him? He used Mexican dimes as quarters for the pay phones.

BAKE TURNER (WIDE RECEIVER): Whenever I'd go out to a speaking engagement, I'd tell the audience that Maynard was so skinny that when he got his leg injured, he'd run over and say, "Bake, you gotta go in for me. I got hit in the calf and it swelled up as big as a broomstick."

16

George Sauer—Split End

SAUER: I didn't want to play football as a kid because my father [George Sr., an All-American and college coach and the Jets' chief scout in the '60s] pushed me into it. My father was head of the Boy Scouts in Waco, Texas, but I quit after the Cub Scouts: I didn't see any sense in getting gold stars for taking out the trash. I began reading a lot in college because the church was on the other side of the campus and I needed an excuse not to go, and that's not facetious. I really didn't like football at Texas that much. I didn't like to block and tackle and all that crap. I just liked to catch the football, but there's more to life than catching footballs.

SNELL: George was very weird. You never knew what he was thinking and he was into meditation. He was quiet, studious, an intellectual. I got the feeling he didn't think anyone on the team could converse with him. He was like from a different aura or level or something. I think what scared George was that he started to like football and felt that he was too anti-football to like this so he better get out. He was really at the top of his game when he walked away from it. [He retired in 1970 at age 26.] Everybody compared him to Raymond Berry, who was then considered the best receiver ever. George had tremendous hands and could run patterns to perfection.

MAYNARD: The thing that helped George become a great receiver was getting contact lenses in 1966 so that he could see what he was trying to catch. His rookie year in '65, lord of mercy, he couldn't catch the ball with a net.

NAMATH: George was a great team man. He never short-changed his responsibility. He'd do everything you'd want a receiver to do, including block. He'd stay after practice and work and work and work.

George just didn't give up on football suddenly. He got out of it because he hadn't liked the way football was being played for a long time. There were dirty players and dirty things being

17

done on the field that hadn't been straightened out, like the illegal head shots receivers were taking downfield. It was unacceptable to George to continue working in that atmosphere.

Matt Snell—Fullback

SNELL: A lot of people don't know this, but even though I went to Ohio State as a halfback, in my junior year I played linebacker and defensive end. [Coach] Woody Hayes moved me to fullback my senior year, but I was more of a defensive player than I was a fullback.

After my senior year, I went to a college All-Star game in Texas—something called the Southwest Challenge Bowl—and I was supposed to play defense. Al Davis was the coach of the National All-Stars, and on the Thursday before the game, he told me that the starting fullback wasn't gonna show up. Al knew I was the only guy there with any experience at fullback and asked if I would play there. I said fine. So I played fullback and gained 169 yards and scored five touchdowns. After that game, I never saw a defensive book again.

In the 1964 draft, the Jets and Giants picked me in the first round which was great because I was from New York, played high school ball in Long Island. The Giants talked to me, but when I looked at who they had there—Frank Gifford, Alex Webster, Kyle Rote, guys I grew up watching play—I didn't think I stood a chance of playing right away. Sonny Werblin really persued me and coach Hayes advised me to sign with the Jets. The AFL was young, most of the organizations were solid. I felt it presented a good future for a guy just starting out in pro football.

The Jets had drafted me as a linebacker, but I gained 117 yards in my first exhibition game so I was officially a fullback. My rookie year I had the most yardage I had as a pro, 948 yards. We had the last game of the season in the bag and I sat out the whole second half because nobody knew I was close to 1,000 yards. I could have easily gained another 52 yards because I'd been having a good day. I didn't even know myself how close I was. That's how important statistics were back then. Now, all these guys can quote you their stats right off their arm band.

ZIMMERMAN: Weeb Ewbank had a great line about Snell's blocking ability. "Snell takes the romance out of the blitz." Snell was a great pass-blocker, but Emerson Boozer became an ever better blocker.

Emerson Boozer—Blocking Halfback

SNELL: I'm responsible for Boozer joining the Jets. We drafted him in the sixth round in '66 and he was leaning toward signing with the Pittsburgh Steelers. [1966 was the last year the AFL and NFL drafted separately.] Weeb brought Em to New York and asked me to talk to him. I told Emerson, "You gotta do what you gotta do, but if the money's nearly right, you got to come and help me out. These guys are killing me. I'm rushing, receiving, doing all the blocking." He decided to sign with the Jets, but played second string halfback behind Bill Mathis. One reason he didn't play much was that he couldn't block. They were really concerned about Namath's protection with his bad knees and Boozer hadn't learned to block at Maryland State. Everybody else blocked for him.

Well, after playing for Woody Hayes, I knew just about all there was to know about blocking so I started working with Em after practice. Thankfully, he had the aptitude for it and he turned into one of the better blocking backs in the league.

As a runner he was very improvisational, kind of like the Earl Monroe of football. He had those natural spin moves and very high knee action. He would get hit in the hole and spin out. I could never do that. As a person, Em was usually quiet, but when he did speak, he sounded almost like a reverend or a preacher. Very authoritative.

ZIMMERMAN: Boozer was having a fantastic year running in '67 before he hurt his knee. I've never seen a guy with better balance, the way he used to bounce and bounce and bounce. He was still a fairly effective runner after the injury, but he didn't

19

have that pinball action to his running. He lost a step and had to do something to survive so he became a sensational blocker.

I'll never forget one scene with Boozer in '67 after he hurt the knee. He was in the locker room with tape on his knee and he was walking around saying, "It should hurt more? Why doesn't it hurt more? It should hurt more than it does." He kept repeating that because he knew how bad it was.

GERRY PHILBIN (DEFENSIVE END): We had the best blocking backfield in football because our backs were taught to block before they ran. Weeb's philosophy was if a back couldn't block he couldn't play on our football team. Snell and Boozer made Joe Namath. They kept those blitzing linebackers like Nick Buoniconti from getting to Joe. I'm talking not only blocking them, but knocking them on their butts. Those guys were devastating.

MAYNARD: We used to call Boozer "cymbals" in workouts because he never seemed to catch the ball. But in a ballgame, I don't remember him missing any.

Chuck Knox—The Offensive Line Coach (1963-1966)

SAM DeLUCA (JETS GUARD, 1964-66, and former team broadcaster for 20 years): Even though he wasn't a Jet coach for the Super Bowl that year, whatever the offensive line accomplished, believe me, it was Chuck Knox who deserves a lot of the credit. Chuck was the guy who really developed the techniques of the way they block today. When I first joined the Jets in '64, Knox asked me what the offensive linemen were doing in San Diego. I told him the only thing we were doing besides the basics was keeping our elbows in so defensive linemen couldn't grab your shoulder pads and grab your elbows. He said, "Well, we've taken it one step further. We not only keep the elbows in, but we extend the forearm and almost lock it."

See, everybody had become a hand fighter. In the early years, people would deliver a blow; they'd hit you inside with a shoulder and a forearm underneath and try to straighten you and then throw you to one side or the other. It evolved that eventually they weren't even making contact. They would come in and grab your shoulder pads. And if you had to keep your hands on your jersey, which is what they originally taught offensive linemen, you didn't have a chance. So Knox said, "If a guy grabs you, you brace, you put that hand out until he removes his hand." And the officials couldn't see your hands because the defensive lineman had his hands to the outside. Chuck helped make Winston Hill and Dave Herman All-Star linemen.

Winston Hill—Offensive Tackle

HILL: Before I was cut by the Colts in '63, I had been told by the Denver Broncos that if Baltimore cut me, to call them. I called them collect, but they wouldn't accept the call. So, I called Weeb and he invited me to the Jets camp. After a few days there, he told me he couldn't use me, but I wouldn't leave. I told him I knew I could make his team, even if I had to stay in New York at my own expense. My grandfather, my great uncle and my father played college ball when everybody said they couldn't make it, and I wasn't ready to accept that I had something I couldn't conquer.

Weeb said okay, I could stay at the Jets' expense if I'd learn how to play center. Well, I centered that ball until I couldn't see. But Sherman Plunkett helped me work on my tackle play, and by '64, I was a regular. Sherman was a great pass-blocker. In fact, my biggest regret about the Super Bowl season is that Sherman wasn't there with me to celebrate the fruits of the victory. Weeb cut him before the season started because he was "overweight." Sherman was over 300 pounds, but they draft guys in the first round over 300 pounds now.

DELUCA: Sherman was an excellent pass protector, but he was fat and lazy. At that point in pro football, guys were lifting weights, but not the way they do today. It wasn't part of the regimen. We didn't know you could bench-press 500 pounds. Sid Gillman instituted it with the Chargers in 1963 and everybody started doing weights after practice throughout the season. I played with Sherman at San Diego that year and I remember going from practice out in the desert—where it would get to 105 or 110 degrees and so dry your shirt would barely be wet— to the weight room. Gillman was there evaluating everyone and Sherman laid down to do bench-presses. I think everyone was starting at 175, just to see what you could do. Sherman couldn't do one, despite the fact that even then he was about 285 pounds. If he played today with the training they have now, he'd be awesome.

SNELL: When Sherman was with the Jets, we kept telling him to get his weight down, but he wouldn't listen. By '68, I think he was up to 325, 330, nobody knew for sure. I remember one time, I think it was '67, we were on a two-week west coast road trip and they surprised Plunkett one morning by bringing in a truck scale to weigh him. The bathroom scales only went to 300. Anyway, he hit about 335 and Weeb kept telling him his legs were going to give out, that he couldn't carry that kind of weight.

A lot guys were pretty upset when Weeb cut him because he was a veteran who everyone liked, especially Winston. I can understand Winston's feeling because Winny is a sensitive person. I called him "Winny the Pooh." He's also not a very complicated person and some of the things that he found interesting or would take seriously, no one else would. One thing he took seriously was practice. He loved to practice, the exact opposite of Verlon Biggs, who hated it. The hotter it was, the more Winston loved practice. Sweat would be pouring out of him and all of a sudden he'd give you one of these war whoops out of nowhere. Ninety degrees and he'd be yelling and screaming, but that's the way he was.

I'm really surprised Winston hasn't made the Hall of Fame because he could dominate. At 6'5", 270 he never lifted weights, but he was strong as a bull.

NAMATH: Winston was the kind of guy you'd love to have as a

father or a brother or somebody to look after your family. The first time I met him was when he came to the hospital after my knee operation after I'd signed with the Jets. This big old body wearing a black leather trench coat came through the door carrying flowers, heh, heh, heh. I'll never forget that. Well, there were so many people coming to visit me, the Jets had set up a room with a bar in it. So here's this big pro football player, one of the first guys I'd met on the team, and I asked him if he'd like to have a drink. He said, "Nah, I don't drink much." I said, "C'mon, Winston, have one drink." So he picked up a bottle of scotch and filled three-quarters of a big water glass and then gulped it down. I swear my eyes almost popped out of my head. I said to myself, "Man, these pro football players are something." But you know what? That might have been the last time I saw Winston take a drink.

ZIMMERMAN: A story came out one season about AFL defensive players voting Winston the number one holder among the offensive linemen. So the writers have to go ask him about it and it's kind of a touchy thing. And so he said, "Just put down that I never held an honest man."

Winston and I got very friendly. One time we were out jogging together and he suddenly said to me, "There's going to come a time when I'm not playing well, when I start slipping. If that happens, I want you to write it and it won't interfere with our friendship." I said, "I'll never write that." He said, "No, you go ahead and write it." I practically started crying.

WALT MICHAELS (DEFENSIVE COACH): Winston Hill hasn't gotten the recognition he deserves for being one of the great offensive tackles. As far as I can see, Winston has got to be the next Jet in the Hall of Fame.

Walt Michaels—Defensive Coordinator

BAKER: Our whole defense was relatively small, particularly by today's standards. We used an unconventional defense because Walt Michaels knew we didn't have guys who could match up and fight it out. You'd look at Kansas City and it seemed every lineman was 6′5″ and you couldn't even see into the backfield with those guys. Walt did a great job with the personnel we had, knowing the guys were small but quick, and putting us into gaps to take advantage of the attributes we had. If we'd had larger guys, we might have played a more conventional defense.

ELLIOTT: Walt Michaels was a terrific defensive coordinator. He had a brilliant football mind. He was a little rough around the edges, but the group of guys he had understood him and he was tough enough to physically challenge you. I was smart enough to know he could probably kick my butt. It was, "Yes sir, no sir," with Walt. I didn't want him on my case. I remember one of Walt's sayings, "Statistics are like a loose woman. You can use them any way you want to."

GRANTHAM: Walt and I never had a cross word in the 10 years I played for the Jets. He and I were just as close as any coach and player could possibly be. I think Walt had full confidence in me to call the right defensive signals at the right time. And none of it was flashed in from the bench. And I think a lot of that was the confidence that Weeb put in Walt as his coach.

JOHN DOCKERY (BACKUP CORNERBACK AND SPECIAL TEAMS PLAYER): If you were screwing up, Walt would come in at half time and go eyeball-to-eyeball with you. Our defensive guys seemed to respond to Walt's toughness and always wanted to play for him. What was amazing was how he was able to put together a secondary made up of all free agents and turn it into part of the best defense in the AFL in '68. And a secondary in the AFL in those days, seems to me, was more important than a secondary in the NFL because there was so much more throwing and, as Joe would point out later, better quarterbacks.

Gerry Philbin—Defensive End

ZIMMERMAN: Gerry was 6′2″, 248, which was undersized for a defensive end even then. He would spin and fake and drive at the offensive lineman. He was mean, too. Someone once asked Philbin what he would be like if he was as big as Verlon Biggs, who was 6'4" and close to 270 pounds. Philbin said, "If I was as big as him, people would have to pay me to let them live."

MICHAELS: Gerry's biggest assets were his instinct, intelligence and his determination to get the quarterback. He'd get such a big pass rush in there, I'd say, "Gerry, did you guess on that thing or did somebody do something to tip you off." He seemed to guess right on pass plays 90 percent of the time. If there was anything you wished it was that Gerry was two inches taller and 15 pounds heavier. He also had chronically bad shoulders, but he compensated for that and the lack of size with great quickness. He made himself into a great player, good enough to be All-AFL for nine years.

PHILBIN: I would never talk to anybody on the other team when I played. I hated it when my teammates went out and socialized with a team prior to a game. I couldn't stand a player doing that. And I'd let him know it. I couldn't be shaking hands with my opponent knowing how much I wanted to go out there and whip him.

If some guys saw me as too intense, well, I'd consider that a compliment. During my playing days, if I knocked the quarterback out of the game, I would have felt really good. If people wanted to call me an animal or sadistic for doing that, that was quite all right.

Verlon Biggs—Defensive End

MICHAELS: Verlon was really the prototypical defensive end that you see today. I'll never forget weighing him in when he came into camp as our number three draft choice out of Jackson State. He was 254 pounds and then went out and ran a 4.65 40-yard dash. I said to myself, "My goodness, look at this guy." Next thing you know, it's halfway into the season and he's at 270 and hasn't lost a step. Verlon was so incredibly strong he could knock an offensive lineman down with his forearm even though Verlon had never lifted weights. He had tremendous leverage and the speed to catch quarterbacks from behind.

BAKER: Verlon was a fairly shy guy when he first came to the team in '65 and so he was always a little misunderstood. He seemed to have unlimited talent, but didn't always seem ready to play. When he was ready, though, he was the most feared guy on the line. Verlon liked to get his big paws into a quarterback's head, and in those days there weren't as many restrictions about going at the head of quarterbacks. I remember one game that year against Boston, he almost ripped Mike Taliaferro's head off.

SNELL: When the game was on the line, Verlon would put out a little extra, and if he did that all the time, I'm sure he would have been a Hall of Famer. He liked to make the big play once or twice during the game when you really needed it, but he couldn't seem to play at that level all the time.

BIGGS: When I first came to the Jets, Dr. Nicholas gave me a physical and announced that I was the strongest player on the team. He asked me if I lifted weights and I said, "No, I just lived." When they timed me for the 40, I ran it in 4.7 and that was just bullshitting around. I could have run it faster than that. My ability came pretty easy to me and I played according to the competition. If we played a team like Kansas City against their good offensive lineman, I got up for the game.

John Elliott—Defensive Tackle

BAKER: If John Elliott wasn't the best defensive lineman in football during that period, he was very close to it. He was up there with [one-time MVP] Alan Page in getting to the QB.

MICHAELS: John didn't have many weak points. He was as fine a pass-rushing tackle as I ever saw. He didn't have the ideal size [6'4", 245], but he was extremely quick. He could go on a pass rush and then break off into run pursuit as fast as anyone.

SNELL: Elliott probably could have been a great linebacker, but he was willing to play anyplace. He had tremendous athletic ability and a lot of upper body strength for his size. Walt Michaels asked him to do a lot of things he wouldn't expect from the other guys on the line because they didn't have Elliott's lateral movement. He and Verlon Biggs would run these tackle-end games. Verlon—who had the strength and the size—would come down the line and grab the tackle and guard, and Elliott would use his speed to go around the outside and put pressure on the quarterback.

Larry Grantham—Linebacker

BAKER: I've got to chuckle when I talk about Larry because he had a most peculiar personality. He was an "I" person. You couldn't talk to him without hearing "I did this," and "I did that." In fact, if our middle linebacker, Al Atkinson, had more of Larry's personality, Al would have gotten much more recognition. Al was the most underrated player in the league. Larry was loud and when he drank the "I" really came out. Most people will tell you he was really hard to take when he drank.

But as a player, he was one of the quickest linebackers I'd ever seen. He was small and nobody ever got a great shot at him. He could duck underneath you and come back around and get away with it. There was no way that I could do the things that he could because I didn't have that quickness. He could do things that were fundamentally wrong. You're always taught to take a guy on with a certain shoulder. He wouldn't even take the guy on, he'd run around him. Say a guy is approaching to block you and if he's coming at your inside, you're supposed to take the guy on with the inside shoulder and close down the hole. Well, Larry would kind of slice inside the guy and still get back to where he was supposed to be. Most players couldn't do that.

JIM TURNER: I'll tell you, Larry was such a great athlete, he could play today, even at 6', 210. When I first joined the Jets in '64, I didn't know what position he played. When I found out he was an All-AFL linebacker, I said to myself, "No way." Then I saw him play and found out he was really quick and smart, like having a coach on the field.

Johnny Sample—Cornerback

SAMPLE: When I signed my first contract with the Colts in 1958, I told [owner] Caroll Rosenbloom that it was amazing to me that there wasn't a black head coach in the NFL. It really bothered me. I talked constantly on radio shows and in newspapers about how prejudiced the NFL was. At that time, other than on the Cleveland Browns, there were only two or four black players on each team. It couldn't be three or five because blacks had to be roommates and those were odd numbers. So I kept getting called in by the Commissioner's office, and they told me not to talk about those things because I was creating a bad image for the league.

I was with the Colts for three years under Weeb. Right before the '61 season, we played an exhibition game in Oklahoma City. I was returning punts and there was one I didn't field. Weeb asked me why I didn't field the punt and I told him it was over my head. Then he said something I didn't like and I said, "Well, fuck you, Weeb." When we got back to training camp, he said, in front of all the players, that he was gonna have to fine me for not handling the punt. I said, "You can't fine me for that. If you're gonna fine me for something, fine me for telling you to fuck yourself. I can accept that. But if you fine me for not handling the punt, I'll leave. I won't play for this team if you do that." So he announced the fine in the meeting and I got in my car and left. I drove home to Philadelphia. Ten days later, the [Pittsburgh] Steelers called and said they'd just traded for me.

I had a good time with the Steelers, even if we didn't win a lot of football games. Was an All-Pro there in '61. I got traded to the [Washington] Redskins two years later and we didn't win any games there either. While I was in Washington, I talked a lot about the way black players were being treated and that there were no black head coaches. I guess I talked about it so much they felt they had to release me before the '66 season.

The reason I always contend that I was blackballed is because after my release I started calling teams for a job and nobody would return my calls. Nobody would even talk to me. Not ONE coach or GM would talk to me and I called all of them. In fact, one assistant coach told me, "There's no sense calling anybody else—nobody's gonna give you a job." That's why I had such a grudge against the NFL, why I hated them so much, why I wanted to win the Super Bowl so badly.

Weeb was the last guy on my list. I figured this guy would never give me a chance because I walked out on him. But Weeb found out that I was calling around to other teams. He knew my abilities as a football player, so he called me up and asked if I wanted to play for the Jets. I said, "I don't know Weeb, we had some problems before." He said, "I don't remember that." I knew better than that because I knew Weeb never forgot anything. In fact, Weeb almost told me he knew I was blackballed. He said, "I found out what happened to you and it's a shame because everybody knows you can still play this game."

SNELL: Johnny was one of a kind; a wild, likable guy who was always bubbly. Not a joker, but always pleasant. Johnny's biggest, biggest problem was women. He loved women. On the road, he'd have them coming and going. A guess there's a flaw in every man's personality and that's what he considered fun. I'm not knocking it, mind you, to each his own. But Johnny took care of himself. He didn't smoke or drink at all.

MAYNARD: I ran against Johnny everyday in practice and I think because of his book [*Confessions of a Dirty Ballplayer*] his reputation has been blown a little out of proportion. Johnny wasn't a dirty ballplayer, but he was the type who would intimidate you. He'd talk to you when you lined up. He'd say, "Hey, you ain't worth a hoot. I don't see how you can play in this league." Johnny would come close to the line of being dirty. If you were on the sideline just a yard in-bounds, he would really hit you.

Jim Hudson—Strong Safety

PETE LAMMONS (TIGHT END): Jim was so tough that right before the '68 season we were sitting in a restaurant in Austin and Hud was bitten by a black widow spider. Those things can be fatal, but Jim's leg just got swollen. I kept telling everybody that Hud was so tough, he lived and the spider died.

WERBLIN: Hudson was bigger than most strong safeties. He was fast, strong and he hit hard. [NFL Commissioner] Pete Rozelle once said to me that he had reports that Hudson took pills. I told him it wasn't so, that if he took pills, he'd be in orbit. He's just one of those wild-eyed Texans; he and Pete Lammons. If I was ever in a fight, I'd want Hudson and Lammons on my side. They're the kind that smile while they kill you.

DAVE HERMAN (OFFENSIVE LINEMAN): If it was recorded accurately, Hudson would rank as one of the top strong safeties ever to play the game. Everybody remembers Jim as being just another guy. There were a lot of us considered average guys because Namath was there and because the guy around the ball is gonna get the most publicity. Hudson did a super job that year, I mean he was the whole defensive backfield. With Sample you didn't know from one minute to the next what he was gonna do. Randy Beverly was just an average player. Bill Baird wasn't very fast. But Hudson brought the whole thing together back there.

ZIMMERMAN: In 1968, Hudson was a combination safetyman-linebacker. He was fast enough to stay with any tight end in the league, and big and strong enough—and a vicious enough tackler—to come up close to the line and work as a linebacker. Sometimes the Jets worked Hudson into what amounted to a pure 4-4 defense, four linebackers and four linemen. People didn't realize his value until after he got hurt in '69 and couldn't play much anymore.

Jim Turner—Place Kicker

TURNER: I set a pro record for field goals in '68 with 34 and it held up until Ali-Haji Sheik of the Giants passed me [with 35] in '83. I think what helped me have such a good year was maturity, getting used to the wind in Shea Stadium—that place was like a death trap for a kicker—and Weeb getting Babe Parilli as the backup quarterback because Babe also became my holder. Babe had been around a long time and everybody respected his knoweldge of the game. As a holder he could get the ball down much quicker. He had the fastest hands I'd ever seen. He moved the spot up a couple of inches towards the center so that when he got the ball the laces would always be facing the goalposts and he wouldn't have to waste time spinning the ball around for me.

I think my major strength as a kicker was my accuracy. I took field goal percentage up to 63 percent after a day when George Blanda and Lou Groza did 49 percent. With some kickers today they should throw out this garbage about field goal percentage. I mean that stuff about Morten Andersen [New Orleans Saints] being a 70 percent kicker. Forget that. He's an indoor kicker and kicking off astroturf. Put him indoors one day and he'll find out what Tony Frisch did when he went from Dallas to an outdoor stadium. He got cut within a year.

Nick Lowery [Kansas City Chiefs] is an exception. I think Nick Lowery is the best kicker in football. Not Gary Anderson [Pittsburgh Steelers] or Morten Andersen or Pat Leahy [Jets]. It's Nick Lowery. But these guys kicking indoors, it's bullshit.

JOHNSON: I was Jim's holder before Babe Parilli joined us, so I knew Jim pretty well as a kicker. Jim really didn't have the leg to kick a ball over 40-45 yards. He had a little punch-kick style that was real accurate, but he didn't get great distance. He had a great year in '68 because the offense always got us in good field position and we were satisfied to take three points.

ZIMMERMAN: Turner was a damn good kicker, but he was a psycho. If you got him in the right mood, he was the greatest guy in the world. He'd talk to you forever. If you got him in the wrong mood, he would just about punch you out. I remember one time a guy on the team went up to him just to talk and Turner says, "Get out of here or I'll blouse your eye." I hadn't heard that expression since the Army. Weeb used to say that Turner was like a crab, that he'd always go sideways.

TURNER: Yeah, I guess I was too serious in those days. If I had it to do all over again, I might not be quite so serious. One thing I was serious about were my kicking shoes. I wore those high-top shoes and I never did like the damn things. For my first two years, I wore low cuts and then Weeb said, "Look, wear the high shoes. If they're good enough for Lou Groza, they're good enough for you." He kept harping on it and finally I just wore them to get him off my back.

But I was particular about my shoes. I liked them clean, I wanted them shined and I didn't want anybody to mess with them because, you know, you only had a couple of pair. I always felt they were my weapon. I didn't think that was abnormal at all.

John Dockery—Harvard Man on Special Teams

DOCKERY: I was a free-agent rookie in 1968, a kid from Brooklyn who played cornerback for Harvard. I'd been cut in August and went to play in Bridgeport. I'd started to think of quitting when with three weeks left in the season, I got a call from Weeb saying the team needed help on special teams. Speedy Duncan of San Diego had run a punt back for a touchdown and the return team was an area they wanted to shore up. I would do anything and everything—receiver, backup quarterback, kicker, you name it.

Once I joined the team, I took a lot of ribbing for being from Harvard. I remember coming into the locker room one day and there was a sign on my locker that read, "Ivy League Practice Today." I figure I'd go along with it and said, "All right, what's an Ivy League practice." Sauer and Maynard were smiling from ear to ear. "Well," they said, "that's touch tackle with pads." But I got along with all the guys, even though they seemed like they were from another world. I mean, it seemed like half the team was from Texas. You needed a dictionary and translator to understand those guys.

The Team Chemistry—Vintage '68

VERLON BIGGS: Going into that season, we had the personnel to go to the Super Bowl, but we still weren't together as a team. So right around our first game we called a team meeting and Johnny Sample kicked it off by saying we were not playing as a complete unit. And everybody got up and said what they really thought about a teammate or anything they wanted to talk about. There was always a little tension or friction around the team because we had a lot of southern guys who weren't used to being in an integrated group. There were a lot of little cliques on the team. The main thing that came out of the meeting was an attitude that, "You don't have to like me as a person, but respect me a player and teammate. I do my job, you do yours and after the season, we'll go our separate ways." We got all that shit out in the open so we could get it out of the way and start playing ball. That's just what we did and we ended up having a lot of fun doing it.

GRANTHAM: We had people who were individuals off the field. I mean we had some real characters. But once we got on the field, we were a very close-knit unit, a team. Now it seems that individualism carries onto the ball field itself.

For example, I could have never played linebacker behind a defensive end like Mark Gastineau. He took such a big outside rush that it put too much responsibility on the outside linebacker. If he sacks a quarterback four-five times, he's had his great game and he's gonna make his million dollars. But he's gonna leave a little old linebacker or somebody standing there behind him looking like a damn first grader. Our linemen would have never done that to us. We knew that if somebody sacked a quarterback it was primarily because a few guys accomplished their assignments allowing somebody else to get free. When I got in trouble was when the defensive linemen took a beating to get me to run free and I didn't sack the quarterback or make the tackle. So it was always a team thing.

BILL BAIRD (SAFETY): We had a lot of experience throughout the team and we were given the freedom to make decisions within the game plan. Weeb's attitude was always, "Hey, you guys are out there playing, what do you think is best?" Players are almost like robots now because coaches do everything for them. Quarterbacks get the plays called for them; there are six coaches on defense calling all the alignments. Consequently, the players just react. In our situation in '68, we'd discuss how we were gonna deal with certain coverages in the huddle. We didn't have to wait for calls from the sideline. With a guy like Larry Grantham and the guys in our secondary, it was like having coaches on the field. Sample, Hudson and myself came up at a time when there were only 33 players on a team and you had to play special teams and positions on offense. In fact, if you included Cornell Gordon, who was our fifth man, our secondary had four guys who were former quarterbacks.

MAYNARD: On that team, everyone seemed to have the attitude that you didn't want to do anything that a teammate would have to get on you about, because, you know, they see things that maybe a coach would never see. I'd rather have Weeb chew me out 10 times than for Pete Lammons or Larry Grantham to chew me out once for not blocking or whatever. On that team, we had a lot of guys who could and would give you constructive criticism. We had such experienced guys in the secondary, they would see things I could do on a cornerback better than me sometimes because I was too busy running my routes.

GRANTHAM: The biggest character on the team was probably Curley Johnson, our punter. Curley was a great mimic and joke teller and kept everybody pretty loose. Curley used to do an imitation of Weeb that was hilarious. He would get down on his knees, pull his uniform shirt out so it reached the floor, and put something under the shirt so his belly really bulged out. Then he'd put his hat on and step up to a microphone at a meeting. Just like Weeb, he'd say, "Now, we're not having a meeting just to have a meeting. Now, we're going to take this trip and we're going to have steak for the pre-game meal. Now, how would you like your steak?" Then imitating Weeb, Curly would start taking orders, "Okay, that's 20 rares, 10 medium rares, five medium wells, four wells. Wait a minute, there's 40 guys on this team. Ah, damnit, somebody didn't vote."

NAMATH: I don't put too much credence into how tight we were as a team. We were tight because we won. It's easy to be incredibly close as a unit and have a lot of camaraderie when you're winning. It takes a special team to stick together and not have any disruptions when you're losing games. Sure, I believe there was an advantage to having so many players from Texas and a few from Pennsylvania, but more important was having so many players who played under great college coaches who instilled a proper winning attitude before we became pros. When I hear that a kid played for four years under a Bear Bryant, or a Joe Paterno, I want him on my side.

DELUCA: The Jets had a good football team that season, not a great football team. When you try to compare people or teams, you've got to think about other teams of that era. Compared to today's players, most of those guys on the Jets wouldn't make it in pro football today, including myself [DeLuca had been an AFL guard with San Diego and the Jets]. On the offensive line, maybe Winston Hill and Randy Rasmussen could play today. On the defense, Gerry Philbin would make it, but he'd be a linebacker. And, of course, Joe Namath would be able to play in any era. Joe was the guy who made the difference for that team, as a great quarterback usually does.

CHAPTER TWO

The $400,000 Gimpy-Legged Quarterback

or
The Legend of Broadway Joe

The salesman's instincts Sonny Werblin had acquired from years in the entertainment business told him it would take one thing to make his Jets and the AFL a money-making winner—a talented quarterback with a star's charisma. Fortunately, for Werblin, the Jets and the struggling league, in 1964 there was just such an athlete playing at the University of Alabama for the legendary coach Bear Bryant. His name was Joseph William Namath.

Namath had grown up in the steel-mill town of Beaver Falls, Pennsylvania, and had become the town's star athlete, excelling in baseball, basketball and football. He was brash, street-smart and colorful, even as a kid, and a sportswriter once said of him: "If Mark Twain had lived in Beaver Falls and had known Joe Namath, nobody would have heard of Tom Sawyer."

As the Beaver Falls High School senior quarterback in 1960, Namath led his team to an undefeated season, impressing college coaches with his throwing arm, running speed, toughness and savvy. When considering which college he would grace with his talents, Namath preferred Notre Dame, but "nearly had a heart attack when I found out they didn't have women." The University of Maryland was his next choice, but he failed by five points to pass the school's entrance exam. Georgia ignored him because they "didn't want any Maryland rejects." So Namath ended up at Alabama, where The Bear became bullish on his new quarterback. "He's the best athlete I've ever coached," said Bryant.

In three years with the Crimson Tide, Namath led his team to a 29-4 record, including three Bowl appearances. He set school records in pass attempts (9,428), completions (230), yards (3,055) and touchdowns (29). He also rushed for 597 yards and 15 touchdowns.

Jets player-personnel director George Sauer, Jr.'s scouting report on Namath read: "He's an outstanding passer with big hands and an exceptionally fast delivery. Good agility and sets up well. Throws the short pass well and can also throw the bomb with great accuracy. Is smart and follows the game-plan perfectly. Is a fine leader and the team has great confidence in him. Will be everyone's number one draft choice."

He was certainly Werblin's. The owner wanted Namath so badly, the Jets traded with the last-place Houston Oilers for the right to select first in the '65 AFL draft. Had Houston drafted Namath, the quarterback might have signed with the NFL's St. Louis Cardinals. The Cardinals were being prodded by their NFL cousins, the New York Giants, to keep Namath out of the clutches of the AFL's New York team.

There was only one negative in Namath's resume—a damaged right knee. During an early-season '64 game against North Carolina State, the knee collapsed while he tried to cut back. Though normally such an injury would demand an immediate operation, Namath played through the pain and the occasional

January 25, 1965. Weeb Ewbank and Sonny Werblin at a press conference after signing The Franchise, torn knee cartilage included. (UPI Photo)

knee-drainings and directed Alabama to a number one ranking and a berth against Texas in the Orange Bowl.

If Werblin, the salesman, still needed to be sold on Namath, then the 1965 Orange Bowl sealed the deal. The bad knee kept Joe Willie on the bench until Alabama fell behind 14-0 in the second quarter. Limping visibly on a heavily-braced knee, Namath exhibited the kind of inspirational leadership that would typify his pro career. He threw two touchdown passes and brought Alabama within one foot of victory when he failed to cross the goal line on the game's final play. Texas won the game 21-17, but Namath was voted the Most Valuable Player.

"You should have seen the way everybody came forward on the edge of their seats when Namath came into the game!" exclaimed Weeb Ewbank. "I never saw anything more exciting than that boy. I see in him the same things I saw in Johnny Unitas."

A few weeks after the Orange Bowl, Werblin stunned pro football by signing Namath to an unprecedented $427,000 contract. (Just to be on the safe side, Werblin spent another $400,000 on three other quarterbacks, including Notre Dame's John Huarte.) To Werblin, Namath was more than worth the risk. The kid possessed star qualities rare in a young athlete—good looks, charm, confidence, and talent. Namath, reasoned the owner, would be the first Jet to bring people into Shea Stadium by sheer force of his personality. Then the media would surely have to take notice. And they did.

Soon Namath was getting as much attention for his swinging, affluent life-style as for quarterbacking the Jets, a situation Werblin heartily encouraged by taking him to New York nightspots and introducing him to celebrities from every area of entertainment. Namath lived in a much-publicized upper East Side Manhattan apartment decorated with a wall-to-wall white llama rug, a huge round bed and a black leather bar. Newspapers, magazines and television shows chronicled how he wore both his hair and his fur coats very long, and that he liked his women blonde and his Johnny Walker Red. He was becoming a big-city folk hero whom the media dubbed "Broadway Joe."

Namath's first two Jets seasons on the field, however, were marked by the resentment of teammates, erratic performances, and more knee operations. Though he was the AFL Rookie of the Year in '65, and threw for over 3,000 yards in '66, it wasn't until his record-setting 4,007-yard season in 1967, that teammates, sportswriters and fans began regarding Namath as a superstar. When he arrived at training camp in 1968, he had matured as a quarterback. He was making the transition from a undisciplined mad bomber who would brazenly force passes into crowded defensive zones to a top gun who could call his own plays, read defenses expertly, and execute a game-plan calling for an efficient ground assault mixed with well-timed, surgical air strikes.

And his on-field mannerisms were becoming as familiar as his off-field image. As Howard Cosell would intone in his familiar cadence, the Jets quarterback was "Joe Willie Namath, the gimpy-legged one from Beaver Falls, Pennsylvania, number 12 in the white shoes. What style, what grace, what a-gil-i-ty." And the Namath style was unmistakable. He would break the huddle and stride slowly but confidently to the scrimmage line, analyzing the defensive alignment for some subtle clue to the opposition's strategy. Reaching the center, his shoulders in a hunch that made his entire body exude cockiness, Namath would slap himself in the chest as if he had locked in a target. After taking the snap, he could be the definition of both grace and klutziness. Tip-toeing quickly back to pass, Namath moved like a dancer. But scrambling out of the pocket when pressured and unable to flex the knee joint, he shuffled along stiff-limbed, looking more like a malfunctioning robot.

Namath possessed an instinctive touch on short passes and incredible arm strength when heaving long bombs. He could hurl bullet-like passes while leaping in the air, throwing off-balance or when tossing from across the field on those difficult sideline patterns. But what made Namath unique among even the great quarterbacks was a release as quick as a gunslinger's draw. He would bring his arm back and hold the ball by his ear while anticipating his receiver's move. Just before throwing he would tap the ball slightly, as if cocking a gun, then rifle it down the field just a nano-second before an onrushing defensive lineman would knock him to the turf.

Namath parlayed his extraordinary athletic ability and his flamboyant image into becoming one of pro football's biggest stars and one of sportsworld's most compelling personalities. The only thing he hadn't achieved at the time Super Bowl III arrived was the media designation of "living legend." But at least one person anointed him as such before the game was even played. "Some people are bigger than life," Sonny Werblin said. "Babe Ruth was bigger than life. And Clark Gable. Frank Sinatra is bigger than life. So is Joe Namath. They can do the darndest things, and it turns out right."

The Namath Image

MAYNARD: When people ask me about Joe's image I tell them, "Whatever you've heard about Joe's ability, you can multiply it. Whatever you've read and heard about his night life, you can divide it." The greatest honor a player can receive is to be voted captain by his teammate, which Joe was in 1968, so that shows you the feeling the team had for him. We all knew that "Broadway Joe" image everybody had of him wasn't the true Joe. A lot of that was publicity. You know, Joe wasn't nearly the swinger people thought he was. We had some guys on our team then that would put Joe to shame. But I won't mention any names because too much time has passed to get in trouble with those guys now.

HUDSON: I was Joe's roommate during the Super Bowl year, and I think the biggest misconception about Joe is what a flamboyant character he was. The press made him out to be that way, but he really wasn't, at least he didn't want to be. Sure, he kept late hours, but a lot of that was caused by the public. I'd been to a lot of places with Joe all over the country and people would stand in line for his autograph while he was having dinner. It would drive you crazy. So he got into the habit of coming back to

Manhattan, watch game films for a while and then go to sleep for an hour or two. Then he'd get up and go have dinner at 10:30, 11 o'clock because he knew people would be off the streets by then.

Another big misconception was that there were games he wasn't ready to play because he was hungover or something. He was ready to play every game. One game late in '68, I think it might have been before the championship game against Oakland, Joe had his family at his apartment and he had dinner with me and my wife and stayed with us that night. But in the paper the next day, there was this story by a reporter, I think it was Jimmy Breslin, who supposedly followed Namath around 'til three in the morning. He wrote about all these bars Joe had gone to and all this drinking he did. Hell, he'd been at my house all night.

SNELL: Joe sort of took everybody by surprise when he started wearing those white shoes—I forget what year it was, probably the year before the Super Bowl—but you could see the game was changing. Heck, everybody was doing different things then. That was about the same time Joe started wearing pantyhose under his uniform. Remember he did that pantyhose commercial? Everyone teased him about the pantyhose, but we were stupid for not wearing them ourselves. They were lightweight and they kept you warm. But Joe didn't care what anybody said.

Joe always had a flair about things. I remember after one of our early games in '68, Verlon Biggs said "I'm not gonna shave again until we win the Super Bowl. So everybody started growing beards and Weeb went along with it. Of course, Joe had to do one better than everybody else, so he comes in with a trimmed "Fu Manchu." He probably went to a barber and had it done. The rest of us had these scraggly beards which we weren't going to shave off until we won. But Joe ended up getting $10,000 to shave it off for a razor commercial. So once again, Namath gets all the attention even though it was Verlon Biggs' idea.

But that southern accent Namath had was so phony. He went to a southern school for four years and all of a sudden he's got an accent. That's like me, a guy from New York, picking up a midwestern accent by going to Ohio State. But everyone thought Joe's accent was so cute. He was a good little southern boy out of Beaver Falls, Pennsylvania.

WERBLIN: In all my career, I have never met a man whose word meant more than Joe Namath's. I can remember when we were trying to sign him. I called Bear Bryant about it. He said, "Do you have his word?" I said, "Yes, but I'd like to have something on paper; I'd feel better about it." Bear said, "You don't need it. If he gave you his word, you don't need the paper."

DICK SCHAAP (from Namath's 1969 autobiography, which he co-wrote, *I Can't Wait Until Tomorrow 'Cause I Get Better Looking Every Day*): Of course, I felt some people would take the book title seriously and condemn Joe as a braggart. He is not. He is a man with a sense of humor, a man who winks at life and winks at himself.

In his serious moments, which are extremely rare, Joe is the antithesis of the braggart. As he reviewed the manuscript of his autobiography, he deliberately edited out anything that smacked of serious immodesty, anything that sounded to him as though he were placing himself on a pedestal.

I'm not going to suggest Joe Namath is a saint; he's not even in field-goal range. He has flaws. I've seen him rude, thoughtless, ill-tempered, impatient, and overly sensitive to criticism. But there are other aspects to Joe Namath that he cannot, or will not, discuss in his autobiography, like his honesty, his generosity, his loyalty to old friends, his respect for his elders, and, of course, his charm, with men and women.

NAMATH: That whole "star" thing with me was a conscious effort on the part of Mr. Werblin, the Jets, and the AFL to get as much publicity for the league as they possibly could. They wanted the country to take the new league seriously and Mr. Werblin be-

lieved in star power selling tickets. When he got into football, Mr. Werblin heard that unwritten rule about everybody being treated the same, that there were no stars, and he thought that was very corny. He knew that wouldn't work. With that contract he offered me, he got more publicity and more attention than he could have bought.

As for all the publicity I received causing misconceptions about me, well, I don't know if there really were any. I know that there were none which existed on our team at the time. My teammates knew what kind of animal I was. I certainly enjoyed my leisure time, but when I came to work, I worked hard. The only misconception that bothered me in the past was the "play-boy image" I had, which can be misconstrued. A "playboy?" I mean, what is a "playboy?" I looked it up one time and found that it meant, "a person who parties to the point of dissipation." I played around, but I didn't party to the point where it hurt my job or hurt me physically. I used to get a little upset about the "playboy" stuff because I don't think enough emphasis had been placed on the seriousness and importance I felt for my job and my team. That always came first. There were times in my immaturity that I allowed all the talk of my off-the-field activi-ties—at the expense of talk about the type of player I was—to bother me. What made it easier was knowing how my team felt about me.

The Teammate Resentments

HUDSON: During our rookie year in '65, some of the veterans may have resented Joe and the money he was getting, but most of them were gone halfway through the season. Besides, as soon as you saw Joe on the practice field, there was no way, unless you were a complete idiot, which some of them were, that you could look at somebody like Joe and not say, "This guy here has what it takes and if we get a few more players around him, we're gonna be in the championship game."

HILL: We had a team meeting a couple of weeks before the '65

45

season because there were a lot of problems with the team. There were some racial problems, players resented Namath's money, a lot of the young guys were having trouble dealing with the New York media. It was a "we gotta get ourselves together" pep-rally kind of talk. Everybody was there, even Sonny Werblin. Sonny said, "You guys aren't protecting Namath. We're not doing anything out there. There's not one indispensable player on this team and if I have to I'll clear out the locker room."

At the end of the meeting, Joe hobbled up with his knee all bandaged and said something like, "I hear some of you guys aren't trying because you're concerned about how much money I got. Well, if you've got a problem, if you don't like me personally, we'll go out and talk about it or fight about it. But don't hate me because of the money I'm making. I got everything I could and you guys would have done the same thing. Besides, it's helped a lot of you get more money." I think that meeting was a major turning point for the organization.

GRANTHAM: Joe never did anything expecting special treatment and he wasn't about to get it anyway because Weeb didn't like that "star system" Sonny Werblin had set up with Joe as the focus of attention. If Joe did anything to break a rule, he knew what the punishment was and he was more than willing to pay the price. All the guys could see that.

SNELL: When Joe came in, right away he was on the cover of *Sports Illustrated* with Broadway in the background. That's where that "Broadway Joe" came from. But Joe's being treated like a big star didn't bother me as much as a lot of people think. It didn't bother me as long as I got what I felt I deserved. People believe Joe and I didn't get along. Let's put it this way, I didn't hang around with Joe, but we got along. If Sonny Werblin wanted to play up that single, good-looking young playboy image, that was all right with me. I knew where I stood with Sonny. But we had some players Joe's first year that it affected a lot. We had a lot of dissension on the team that year. Later on, if anyone resented Joe's star status, I think it was Gerry Philbin. I remember him asking for a raise based on what Namath was getting. Management told him "Namath is one thing, you're a defensive end, Gerry, and you're something else." He sort of resented that his whole career.

RANDY RASMUSSEN (OFFENSIVE GUARD): I think all the money and publicity Joe received was resented by some of the guys. But I think most of us understood that Joe was the guy who put people in the seats and made it possible for the league to sell those commercial spots on television for big numbers. If you really understood football, which most guys did, how could you resent it? But I don't think it hurt the team. We were the kind of team that differed about a lot of things, but put it behind us and played hard every Sunday.

JIM TURNER: I remember that big controversy at the beginning of pre-season in '68 when Joe sat out a couple of exhibition games because he supposedly wanted $3,000 per game to play. I sent him a telegram—I believe he was playing in a golf tournament at Tahoe South Shore—in total support. I said, "I'm with you, Joe, in whatever you're doing."

We went to play an exhibition game in Alabama and the 30,000 people there were all there to see Joe. They didn't come to see Jim Turner or Weeb Ewbank. So if Joe asked for a few thousand dollars, he deserved it. And if anybody resented it, they were wrong because whatever fruits of victory we received, we got them because of Joe Willie. We got in there as a team, but you don't do it without a quarterback. There are a lot of guys, a lot of phonies around who call themselves stars and such, but I've only played with one superstar and that was Joe Namath.

ZIMMERMAN: The real story was that the team was divided about Namath, especially when Sonny Werblin was there before '68. Snell and Philbin resented him. Wouldn't you resent a guy that got special treatment? Goes out drinking with the owner and gets drunk, comes in for the game hung over and throws five, six interceptions and doesn't get punished? I mean wouldn't you be pissed off about that? They had a good enough team to win in '67, even with Emerson Boozer getting hurt in the second half, but Namath was throwing all those interceptions. In those years, he was a guy who kept both teams in the game.

The problem was he wasn't studying enough, training enough or sacrificing. He was screwing around and getting away with it. I remember [New York *Daily News* sportswriter] Dick Young arguing with an old referee one day and Young was saying that when you've got a star like Namath, you've got to have a different standard for him. Sonny Werblin had made Young his pipeline, which was smart because Dick was the best columnist in New York; he was number one. And Sonny fed him material and Dick never took a shot at the Jets until Sonny was gone. Then Dick went 180 degrees and was Namath's worst enemy in the press.

Matt Snell didn't like Namath. I once asked Snell during the Super Bowl year about Namath's leadership and he said, "He doesn't lead anybody. He does his job, he completes passes. I do my job, I run the ball. That's all there is to it." A lot of it with Snell was jealousy.

But Namath got along great with the rest of the black guys on the team. Winston Hill was a big supporter. Winston thought Joe was a great guy, a fine human being. Namath was very good on racial stuff because he grew up playing with black guys in grade school in Beaver Falls. He was very smart that way and was very aware of the black/white history on the Jets. He would go into the dining room and there'd be a table filled with black guys and Namath would walk over and sit himself down in the middle of them. And then pretty soon another white guy would come over and then it would be an integrated table. He did that all the time. It happened too many times to be accidental.

The Namath Knees

DR. NICHOLAS: I did all the operations on Joe's knees, which became the most famous knees in the history of sports. With all the media exposure Joe got, his knee problems became well known all over the country. [Sportswriter] Dick Young wrote a piece in *Look* magazine about me treating the team's knee injuries and they called it, "Those Weak-Kneed Jets." At the beginning of Namath's career, I didn't feel much pressure operating on him. But by '68, the team was blossoming and every time Joe had an injury it was headline news. I'd never seen headlines in my life about athletic injuries like we had then with Joe. But you know what, Joe's injuries really stimulated an interest in sports medicine. At that time, it wasn't a specific science. With all the media exposure that Joe received, his knee problems became well-known all over the country. It all contributed to the awareness of the anterior cruciate ligament of the knees and how they should be treated.

The cruciate ligament he tore in his right knee at Alabama in 1964 was the same kind of serious injury that later happened to Matt Snell, Joe Klecko, Mark Gastineau and Bernard King, when he was with the New York Knicks. Those things usually have to be operated on right away, but Joe played the next two months of the college season and in the Orange Bowl with the injury. Really hard to believe. After we signed him, they had a big press conference at Toots Shor's restaurant. I'd never seen Joe before, but Weeb asked me to take a look at him. I know it sounds crazy, but in those days they signed players without examining them first. So I took Joe into the bathroom and examined his knee. When we came out, I said to Weeb, "You better get another quarterback." They had also signed John Huarte from Notre Dame and when I examined him I found he had a bad shoulder. He ended up having to quit football.

I operated on Joe the next week, he was in a cast for two months and then rehabilitated all summer. He played in 1965 with a bad knee because the operation couldn't repair the ligament. It was irreparable at that time because they didn't operate right away. That's when we designed the "Lenox Hill [Hospital] Brace" which became widely used all over the world. Anyway, because Joe couldn't set up on his right leg properly, he quickly developed tendonitis in the left knee. Then, to take the pressure off his left knee, his right knee got worse, and after the '66 season, we had to operate on that one again. Then in '68, we had to repair a tendon in his left knee, and in '71, he tore the left cruciate, but was able to play five more years after that operation.

Joe was remarkable because he not only had a tremendous pain threshold, but had a very philosophical attitude about his injuries. He'd say, "This isn't cancer, it's just a bad knee." He once went to Vietnam and saw guys in hospitals all shot up and he'd say, "Man, thank God all I have to cope with is a knee problem." Joe had a wonderful capacity to adjust to his problems.

You know, I guess it's ironic, but if Joe had been operated on immediately in '64, knowing what we now know about knee injuries today, Sonny Werblin would have never signed him. His knee would have been in better shape, but he would have had to sit out the rest of the season and at best would have been a fourth- or fifth-round draft pick. Nobody would have taken a chance on a quarterback who had been operated on in October. So if Joe hadn't kept playing in that '64 college season, football history would have been drastically different.

DELUCA: Psychologically, it was a tremendous feat for Namath to go out there for a game with those old man's knees. It's tough enough out there when you can go 100 percent. When you can go only 50 percent you've got to be thinking: "How will I do? Will I get hurt because I can't go all-out?" It has to affect you. But I'll say this for Joe, I admired him for it. Not once did I ever hear him complain about the pain or use his knees as an excuse when he had a bad day.

EWBANK: If Joe's knees were better, we probably would have used more play-action and roll-out stuff. But if Joe had to do a lot of twisting and turning, particularly early in the season, why his knees would swell up. I'd watch Doc Nicholas put that needle in Joe's knee to drain it and I'd have to leave the training room. I really felt sorry for the guy. A lot of guys wouldn't even play with injuries like that.

DR. NICHOLAS: I was always scared to death that Joe might hurt his arm the way baseball pitchers do when they alter their motions after a leg injury. You know, like how Dizzy Dean's career fizzled after getting hit in the toe with a line drive. But that never affected Joe, even with the two bad knees. We did some studies on Namath and Unitas and found that because they had a slouch or a "round back," when they set up to throw, their hand would only go back to their ear. That's what accounted for their quick release. They never got the arm way back the way most pitchers do and that's why Joe never had a bad arm. A guy with a round back is less likely to get a bad shoulder.

We also watched Joe on film and learned a lot from studying his quickness dropping back and his awkwardness running forward. He looked like two different athletes and that's because the injuries had cut down the mobility of the knee when he tried to spin and rotate. And the way we had to brace his knees, he couldn't turn the leg in or out; he couldn't make an outside or inside cut. But it enhanced his ability to go straight back and forward. The braces made him learn an economy of movement. He already had the great arm, the hand-eye coordination, and the ability to read the defenses. Before Joe used the Lenox Hill Brace I designed, they didn't think you could brace a knee and retain enough mobility to play a sport. Joe proved you could do it. And if Joe got hit head on, with those steel braces on, the defenders felt it more than Joe did.

Namath's Talent

EWBANK: People have asked me if I was ever worried about Joe not sticking to the game plan in the Super Bowl and throwing the ball a lot because it was a showcase. I never doubted Joe would stick to the plan. Joe was flashy and had a lot of confidence in his ability, but he wasn't a showoff on the field. He was a team player. I would hear newspaper guys tell him what a great day he had and Joe would say, "Well, gee, anybody can throw the ball with the protection I had." He was always good about giving a guy credit and the offensive line loved him. They always gave extra effort to protect him.

And since I coached Johnny [Unitas] at Baltimore, I'm always asked to compare him and Joe. I remember a woman saying to me one time, "You know, I always get my money's worth on my ticket just watching Joe take the ball from center and go back and set up. He's just so graceful. And that was one of the differences. Despite the bad knees, Joe was such a great athlete he seemed to glide. John would kind of pound when he ran with the ball. And when John threw, he would come back up into the pocket and would follow through like a baseball pitcher on the mound. He'd follow through so hard with his arm and wrist that sometimes his fingers would hit a helmet or a jersey or something and he'd hurt his hand. Joe dropped back deeper because he didn't come back up into the pocket as well. But he could drop deeper because he had that quick release, an incredibly strong arm and got his hips into the throw. I don't think anybody could throw a 20-yard out pass as well as Joe.

NAMATH: One thing I had that I haven't seen from anybody since, except maybe for Joe Montana, is footwork. I had excellent footwork and great feet to go with it. It wasn't something I developed to compensate for my knee injuries, it was a God-given ability. Coach Bryant used to say I was as quick as a cat. I really took pride in my quickness and agility. The best passer I've ever seen without quick feet is Dan Marino, which is kind of ironic because people always compare his style of throwing to mine.

HUDSON: Not only did Joe have more natural ability than anybody I'd ever been around, he had two other things that make a great player—instinct and intuition. And he was as tough mentally as anybody I ever knew. You put all those things together with an understanding of the game and you've got yourself a superstar.

MAYNARD: People talk about Joe's arm and release and everything, but I think Joe's greatest ability was his anticipation, especially anticipating all the receiver's moves. That's something we worked on for 20, 30 minutes a day each week for years. I think we only had one busted play in eight years. Joe got rid of the ball so quick, our offensive lineman could go get a hamburger. It didn't matter if a guy blitzed. Joe could release the ball when the defenders were still two yards behind the line of scrimmage. I was always amazed at the way he could throw with a flick of the wrist even when he was off-balance. And he could drop back quicker than a lot of guys could move forward. But Joe didn't have the greatest running style with them knee braces on. He kinda looked like a horse that hobbles.

Joe and I had a great understanding. When he first came to the Jets, I told him, "You make me look good and I'll make you look good. We're in this together. I know sometimes you throw off balance. I'll never knock you for a bad pass." Right off the bat, we had a great thing going.

JOHN SCHMITT (CENTER): Well, you know the old football joke: "No two men can be closer than the center and his quarterback, ha, ha, ha. If the QB pulls out too early before the snap, the center doesn't have kids the rest of his life, heh, heh." But seriously, Joe and I were great friends even though I didn't hang out with him socially. I was married and had three children. Joe was single and had 28 girlfriends. I couldn't say to my wife, "Hey, honey, I'm just gonna go into the city and visit with Joe tonight and we're going to the library." I mean, she knew that wasn't going to happen. But Joe and I had a very special understanding, an unspoken relationship. I could look into his eyes and know whether he was hurt bad enough for us to take a time out. I knew when I needed to talk to him to calm him down.

I used to get asked a lot about whether the offensive line felt any added pressure to protect Joe because of his knees and everything. Well, you always feel pressure to protect the quarterback because when you're an offensive lineman, you're graded on every play. But even though we didn't want to admit it, you'd look at the films and see that we did block better for Joe than we did for the other quarterbacks. It must have been a subconscious thing. Every guy on the line must have felt, "Hey, I can't let Joe get hit or he'll get hurt." It wasn't that we didn't love the other guys. It was just a feeling that you would bite a defensive player's gonads off before you'd let him get to our meal ticket.

RASMUSSEN: On the offensive line, we felt that if we could give Joe two to two and a half seconds, he had like an 80 percent chance to complete the pass. To me, the more impressive thing about Joe was his ability to read defenses and know how to exploit a weakness. And he was constantly talking to his wide receivers, especially Maynard and Sauer. You know, the guys up front said very little in the huddle so we just listened to what the receivers were saying. They'd come back and tell Joe what they could do on certain cornerbacks. And when you heard chatter like that going on, I always felt, "Man, we got this game under control."

GRANTHAM: Joe certainly helped the defense's confidence because we knew that no matter what the score was or what point in the game it was, all we had to do was get the ball back for Joe and he'd make something happen. Sometimes it wasn't good 'cause he could throw interceptions. But most of the time it was something positive. So it gave us a little more incentive to get the ball back in critical situations when we were down. You know, I'd rather have Joe Namath at quarterback when we were down 10 or 14 points than have somebody else and be up by seven.

ZIMMERMAN: If Namath had applied himself a bit more, he

would have been a truly great quarterback. But if you look at his whole career, he was hot and cold; an erratic quarterback. He didn't dedicate himself enough to always be in top physical condition. But his approach to the game was very intelligent. He and Clive Rush would talk strategy on the plane all the time. Namath really cared about the intellectual aspects of football.

DOCKERY: Maybe Joe's training regime wasn't always the best because of his social life, but he studied the plays, watched films and worked hard in practice. More importantly, he was a great competitor and a leader. If you ever wanted a guy on your side, it was Joe. You talk about having guys with you in foxholes or in alley fights or in a tough football game, Namath was the kind of guy you'd want around. You knew he'd be courageous and gutsy and tough. What else could you ask for in a teammate?

Joe was a guy with a golden arm, who could also lift the team on the strength of his personality, emotion, and confidence. I mean, it was like riding the crest of a wave. Even when he was stopped and the defense was coming on the field, he'd say, "Just hold them and I'll get it back." And it wasn't just words—every quarterback says that—because more often than not, he did.

DELUCA: Namath was simply the best. I still think he is the best ever. Well, wait, let me amend that. I don't think anybody's better than Dan Marino. But Marino has all of Namath's qualities. Up until Marino, Namath was the best.

CHAPTER THREE

The First Steps Toward the Super Bowl

The 1968 New York Jets and their burgeoning legion of fans—attendance in 1967 had been up 22,000 from the previous year for an average of 62,433 per game—would find out quickly whether or not their team was Super Bowl material. Not only would the Jets have to play their first three games on the road (in yearly deference to the baseball Mets, whose status as Shea Stadium's primary tenants kept the Jets off the grass until baseball season concluded), but the opener would be against the Kansas City Chiefs, the AFL's representative in Super Bowl I and arguably the league's most talented team.

With the largest crowd in Kansas City watching, Joe Namath and Don Maynard (who would catch eight passes in the game for 203 yards) put on an aerial display that included first half touchdowns of 57 and 30 yards, and gave the Jets a 17-3 half-time lead. But an 80-yard Noland Smith punt return and two Jan Stenerud field goals following Jets turnovers brought the Chiefs to within a point. The teams then traded fourth-quarter field goals, making the score 20-19.

There were just over five minutes remaining in the game when the Jets were faced with a third down and 11 on their own four-yard line. Failure to get the first down would mean punting

Don Maynard, a survivor
of the New York Titans,
became a top flanker for
the Jets. (AP/Wide World
Photos)

There were two crucial wins that qualified the Jets for Super Bowl III.
The first was a 20-19 win over the Kansas City Chiefs. Here Don Maynard catches a Joe Namath pass in full stride for 56 yards and the Jets'
first touchdown. Kansas City defensive back Goldie Sellers comes up
empty-handed. (AP Wirephoto)

out of the end zone and excellent field goal position for the Chiefs. But Namath, voted co-captain by his teammates prior to the game, masterfully engineered a drive that ran out the clock, supplying a confidence boost that would carry the team for the entire season.

Not that the year didn't have its share of shaky moments. Sandwiched around a thrilling come-from-behind 23-20 victory over San Diego (in front 63,786 fans, the biggest crown in AFL history), the Jets blew games to Buffalo (37-35) and Denver (21-13), two of the league's worst teams. The good news was that Namath threw four touchdown passes against Buffalo and passed for 341 yards against Denver. The bad news was he threw five interceptions in each loss. "It seems we don't get up for the little ones," said George Sauer.

They needed to get up for a big one the following week against the Houston Oilers, the Jets' main competition for the Eastern Division title. A safety, a touchdown and a two-point conversion (they had an option in those years) gave the Jets a 10-0 lead at half time, but the Oilers scored two second half touchdowns and led 14-13 with a bit over four minutes to play. Again displaying a comeback habit that must have turned Jets fans into nail-biters, Namath produced a clutch touchdown, marching them 79 yards to the winning score with 48 seconds left. "I don't know what it is," said Sauer, in another brief, yet perceptive post-game analysis, "but we don't catch fire until we get into trouble."

The Jets would get little trouble from Boston (five interceptions by the defense in a 48-14 win), Buffalo (a record-tying six Jim Turner field goals in a 25-21 victory), and Houston, a 26-7 triumph which gave New York a three-game lead and all but wrapped up the division title before Thanksgiving. There would be no time for a pre-turkey day letdown, however, with a road game to play against the Oakland Raiders.

Over the AFL's brief history, the Jets and Raiders had become bitter rivals, a football version of the Jets and the Sharks. The field battle was like an alley gang-fight and helmeted players hurled themselves into each other as if they were human switchblades. During the late '60s, these teams liked each other about as much as conservatives enjoyed the company of Vietnam War protesters. The slogan of the evil-looking, silver and black clad Raiders was "Pride and Poise," but to the Jets it was more like "Pillage and Punish." One famous episode occurred during the 1967 meeting when Oakland's 6'8", 280-pound defensive end Ben Davidson cracked Namath's cheekbone on a late tackle.

Besides the brutal hitting, like most Jet-Raider affairs, this would be another *mano-a-mano* between Namath and Daryle Lamonica. In other words, there would be footballs flying all over the field. By half time, the Raiders led 14-12 on two Lamonica touchdown passes and there had been 11 penalties totaling 149 yards. Each team scored a touchdown before Joe Willie went wild, hitting Maynard on two straight bombs covering 97 yards for a 26-22 lead. A Jim Turner field goal made it 29-22, but Lamonica quickly tied it with a 22-yard scoring pass to Fred Biletnikoff. Namath refused to be outgunned. He drove the Jets into field goal range where Turner hit a 21-yarder with 68 seconds left, giving the Jets an apparent 32-29 victory.

Incredibly, the Raiders scored two touchdowns—one on a 43-yard pass and the other on a fumble of the subsequent kickoff—in the last 50 seconds to win 43-32. Even more incredibly, millions of television viewers missed the stunning turn of events when at 7:10 P.M., NBC switched from the game to a special presentation of *Heidi*, a programming decision that has lived in infamy for sports fans. (As of early 1989, *Heidi* was ranked in viewership as the number 12 most-watched television movie of the previous 25 years.) New York fans not listening to the game on radio didn't receive the bad news until about 8:30 P.M.

NBC may have suffered some short-term negative effects from the game, but the Jets certainly didn't. Mentally writing off the "Heidi game" loss as a fluke, they coasted into the AFL championship game—and a rematch with the 12-2 Raiders (who beat the Chiefs in a playoff for the Western Division crown). They produced four successive victories to finish the year at 11-3.

On a cold, damp and windy afternoon, three days before the new year, 62,627 fans packed Shea Stadium for the Jets' first championship appearance. A few hundred thousand more huddled around radios in their homes since these were the days when home games—even title games—weren't televised by the networks. And they missed a classic.

The game was tied at 13 early in the third quarter, when Namath went into ball-control mode and directed a time-consuming 80-yard drive, culminating in a 20-yard touchdown pass to Pete Lammons. Never wanting to be outdone by Namath, the mad bomber Lamonica dropped back with 11 minutes left in the game and hit Biletnikoff on a 57-yard pass, giving the Raiders a first down on the New York 11. For the second time in the game, the Jets defense toughened, forcing another Blanda field goal and leaving the Raiders four points behind.

The Jets took possession on their own 22 needing another long drive to all but end the contest. But suddenly, Namath's evil twin emerged, the one from those Buffalo and Denver debacles, and he threw an interception on the first play. Cornerback George Atkinson, who was covering Don Maynard, returned the ball to the Jets' five, and one play later, Pete Banaszak rumbled into the end zone, giving the Raiders a 23-20 lead with just over six minutes remaining.

But Namath displayed an affinity for the dramatic comeback all season. After hitting Sauer for a first down at the Jets' 42, he and Maynard went right back at Atkinson and connected on a 52-yard pass that put the ball on the Raiders' six. Just one play later, Maynard corralled a Namath bullet in the back of the end zone. Turner's extra-point made it 27-23 with about six minutes left in the game.

With Lamonica now passing on every play (he would throw 47 passes for 401 yards), the Jets pass rush became manic in its pursuit of the Oakland quarterback. The defensive line forced Lamonica to hurry passes, and though Oakland entered Jets territory, Verlon Biggs ended the Raiders drive with a fourth-down sack that pushed the Raiders out of field-goal range. Oakland got the ball back, however, with three and a half minutes remaining and in desperate need of a touchdown. By the two-minute warning, Lamonica had connected on 24 and 37-yard passes, putting the ball on the Jets' 24. On the following play, the quarterback hurled a swing pass behind running back Charlie Smith and the ball fell for an apparent incompletion. But alert Jets linebacker Ralph Baker realized the throw was a lateral—which made it a free ball— and quickly scooped it up to end the last Oakland threat.

Less than two minutes later, the Jets were AFL champions and two weeks away from their date with destiny.

The Turning Point

GRANTHAM: It's very rare that the first game of the season can be called a "turning point," but I think our opener against Kansas City that year gave us the confidence to believe we could go all the way. We were up 20-19 with about six minutes left. Problem was, we had that third and 11 and we were down on the Chiefs four. If we don't get out of that mess, they kick a field goal and win the game, right? Then Joe hit Maynard on a slant-in, Don broke a couple of tackles and got the first down. After that, Joe just controlled the clock all the way down the field and we won by a point. It just boosted everyone's confidence.

SNELL: I remember that game vividly because of that last drive. If felt like we controlled the ball for 10 minutes. [Chiefs coach] Hank Stram said after the game that he could never have believed anyone could do that to his team.

TURNER: Weeb said before the game that it would be a big test of how far we would go that year. I remember it very well because Jan Stenerud kicked four field goals and I kicked two, the last one put us ahead 20-16. At that point, it was the biggest field goal of my career.

MAYNARD: It was a big game, not only because we beat Kansas City, but because the day prior to the game we had elected Joe co-captain, and in the first game he led us to a victory. On that last drive, we told Joe that it was up to him to take us all the way and he did it. The team had a lot of confidence in Joe after that.

NAMATH: We were coming off a season in '67 that we felt really got us ready for '68. We knew we were starting to jell as a team and that we were doing things with the passing game that no one else had ever done in football. Our defense was improving constantly, and so, yes, as odd as it is to call the first game of the season "pivotal," beating Kansas City that day in their own stadium, especially holding the ball the last six minutes, certainly gave us all a tremendous amount of confidence.

SAMPLE: You know why most guys say the Kansas City game was the turning point. Because man-for-man, compared to any roster in the AFL or the NFL, the Chiefs probably had more ability, more talent than anybody. I mean, they were in Super Bowl I, won 12 games in '68, and won the Super Bowl in 1970. You talk about Ernie Ladd and Bobby Bell and Ed Budde, I mean those guys were awesome. They tilted the field when they walked on it. You know what I mean? They made the field rotate. So when we beat them on opening day, that had to make us feel pretty good about ourselves.

I think another key game was the fourth game against San Diego because we had just been upset by Buffalo. Joe puts us up 23-20 with a minute and a half to go and then the Chargers started driving down the field. Lance Alworth had caught nine or 10 passes on me and by the end of the game I was thinking, "This guy is eating me alive." Then John Hadl threw a long sideline pass and I intercepted it on the four and ran it back almost 40 yards. I was so tired I was hoping someone would tackle me.

The Namath Debacles

NAMATH: Buffalo. Heh, heh, heh. Before I went into that game, a friend asked me how I thought we'd do. Well, we were 19-point favorites. I said, "I tell you what, we have the best defense in the league, a darn good offense, they have a rookie quarterback. I don't know how they're gonna score." When I got back Sunday night after the game, my buddy said, "Joe, I figured out how they're gonna score. You're gonna throw five interceptions." At any rate, after my fourth or fifth interception, Babe Parilli said to Weeb, "Hey, Weeb, want me to go in and give the kid a break." Weeb said, "Hell, no. He got his ass in it, let him get his ass out of it."

ZIMMERMAN: You know why Namath threw those five interceptions against Buffalo [third game of the season]? That team had his number. He hated Buffalo. It was his least favorite place to play. He didn't like Memorial Stadium because the winds were so bad there. Then two weeks later, he throws five more against Denver at Shea because the pass protection broke down and a couple of rookie defensive backs were all over Sauer and Maynard.

NAMATH (in '69): I don't think I ever played any worse than in that game against Denver in '68. Even though I completed 20 passes, which was my season high, I knew that I'd cost us the game. In the locker room after the game, I made only one comment to the writers. I said, "I stunk," and I was being kind to myself.

NAMATH (in '89): The problem with that Denver game was that it had rained all week and we had to practice indoors. We couldn't pass or do anything and Weeb was worried about our timing. I said, "Weeb, don't worry about it. We'll be all right." Well, Weeb was right. Our timing was way off. The plays were there, but I couldn't hit anybody. We couldn't do anything right.

SAMPLE: I never will forget that Denver game. Joe wasn't the only one who had a bad game. I didn't play well either. I'd worn a black silk suit to Denver, but after the game, I cut it up, left it in the locker and wore my warm-up suit back home on the plane. I said to myself, "If this is going to bring me this much bad luck, I don't want to see it again."

HUDSON: I think Joe came into his own as a great quarterback after the Denver game, and Walt Michaels had a bit of an impact. Walt knew Joe and I were friends and roommates, and since I'd been a quarterback at Texas, I guess he thought I could get through to Joe. Walt came up to me one day at practice and said, "You need to tell your roommate how to be a quarterback." I said, "Shit, you tell him, Walt." He said, "Hell, I can't tell him. All he needs to know is that every time he goes out there, the other quarterback is gonna try to outdo him, so he doesn't need to do anything. All he has to do is have some more patience, not force the ball so much, and let the defense force the other team into mistakes. Tell him to just let the defense help him win the football game and he'll be the greatest quarterback of all time." After Joe and I talked about that, he went about six, seven games in a row without throwing a touchdown pass, but we won every game handily. I think we all learned a little bit about football and about our team at that point. We had a good defense, but nobody realized it.

NAMATH: After those games, Walt Michaels was very frustrated. He comes up to me and says, "Joe, look, we go into these games and we've got everything going for us. So what the hell are we doing taking chances. We've got to approach a game like that with a conservative attitude." And I listened to Walt and he was right. My only comment to Walt when he got through was, "Hey, Walt, next time tell me before the game." After those games, I did consciously give it a more conservative effort. I took fewer chances and relied more on our team. I went six straight games without completing a touchdown pass, but they were beautiful games for me because we won.

ZIMMERMAN: From the Denver game until the end of the season, Namath threw only five touchdown passes in nine games and had, I think, one interception every 42 passes, which was the best in the league. We were all writing stories about what was wrong with Namath, he wasn't throwing touchdowns anymore. Well, what happened was the defense got good and he realized he didn't have to put 30 points on the board every week. He could get the team in good position for Jim Turner to kick all those field goals. He realized he could run a basically conservative offense and that's what he did. We were too stupid to figure that out.

The "Heidi Game"

JIM TURNER: Weeb didn't like or trust anything about the Raiders when we were in Oakland. He always felt they were cheating, that they bugged the locker rooms, so we couldn't say as much before the game. If a helicopter went over, Weeb would stop practice in case the helicopter was photographing us.

HUDSON: The "Heidi game" was just another typical Oakland-Jets game out there. Plenty of penalties, most of them called on us. [The Jets were flagged for 13 penalties and 145 yards, both club records at the time, and five were for grabbing the face mask.] I don't know if it was fact or fiction, but back in those days it felt like you had to beat about 15 or 16 players because the referees always seemed to call the game favorably for Oakland. And it wasn't just us saying that, everybody felt that way. I don't know if [Raiders' owner] Al Davis was paying the refs or what, but he was Commissioner long enough [three months in 1966] to hire all of 'em. And it seemed as though that crew was always there.

Those refs certainly got me that game. Kicked me out in the third quarter. We were up 19-14 and I think they had a third or fourth and one deep in our territory [it was actually a third and five from the Jets' 13] and we were trying to hold them to a field goal. They ran nothing but a little old sweep to Hewritt Dixon, and as strong safety, I was the force on the play. I made the tackle after he got a couple of yards. All of a sudden, I heard a little thing—bing!—hit my helmet. It was that little weight they have on the end of the penalty flags and the referee was pointin' at me, hollering "face mask, face mask." Then Hewritt and I started hollerin'. He was saying he was gonna whip my ass and I was yellin' I was gonna whip his ass, and flags started flying all over the place. I didn't even come close to Hewritt's face mask. In fact, we went over the film and it showed there was no face mask involved. Even Hewritt told me after the game that it wasn't no face mask.

Anyway, I got booted out of the game and they ended up getting the go-ahead touchdown [before Earl Christy's fumbled kickoff was recovered and turned into the second TD] when Lamonica hit Charley Smith with a pass in what would have been my area.

GRANTHAM: I got hurt on the play that got Hudson kicked out of the game. We'd both hit Dixon on a little swing pattern. I hit him low so I know damn well I didn't grab his face mask. All of a sudden, there's a flag laying on my shirt. And I said, "Hudson, what the hell happened." And the referee comes running up and yells, "Face mask." And I said "Hudson, you son of a..." And Hud said, "I ain't touched him around the face." Meanwhile, I'm laying there with a pinched nerve in my neck. And I had to go to the hospital for X-rays, so I missed the end of the game.

So I'm on the X-ray table in the emergency room and some nurse comes running in there and tells me the Jets have just scored to take the lead. I was really confident we'd won the ball game, but never found out the final score while I was in the hospital. It wasn't until I got to the airport and saw all the long faces that I found out what happened, like what Hudson did on his way out of the stadium. He gave the Oakland fans the bird. I remember Wendy Hudson, who was married to Jim at the time, saying, "Can you believe it? My husband gave everybody the finger on national television." That must have gotten everybody in the right frame of mind for *Heidi*.

SAMPLE: After the game, I flew from Oakland back to my home in Philadelphia because I had some important business. My father picked me up at the airport early Monday morning and said, "You guys played a great game yesterday and I'm so proud of you the way you won." I said, "What are you talking about?

67

Proud of what? What are you joking around like this for? We lost the game." He said, "You WHAT? No way you lost that game. You were winning 32-29 with a minute to go. It was almost over and they put *Heidi* on so I went to sleep." I had to tell him that we'd lost 43-32 and that the Raiders had scored two touchdowns in the last 50 seconds.

EWBANK: I called my wife Lucy after the game and she'd thought we'd won. She'd been watching TV and the danged thing went off with a minute to go when we were ahead.

DICK CLINE (NBC Broadcast Operations Control Supervisor in 1968): The day of that Jets-Oakland Game, I was the supervisor on duty in New York, the guy in charge of making sure everything got on the air at the appropriate time. So I was the guy who pressed the button to switch from the game to *Heidi*, the special presentation that was pre-empting "Walt Disney's Wonderful World of Color" that Sunday evening. I gave the order for the execution, so to speak.

During the week, at a meeting of our programming department, we decided that come 7:00 P.M., we would cut away to *Heidi* even if the game was not over. We'd had that provision a couple of times before, but nobody was really worried about it because the games never ran long. In those days, the games weren't consistently over three hours like they are today, and if one did run long, normal strategy was that the show would be joined in progress. We didn't slide the network programming like they do now. *Heidi* was responsible for that.

Anyway, *Heidi* was being sponsored totally by Timex and the network's primary concern was to get that show on at seven because Timex had paid for all the time. You treated a sponsor like that very carefully because you wanted them to come back. And since it was "only" AFL football and nobody was really sure how many viewers watched anyway, it seemed like the thing to do. Even if the ratings had been better, I don't think we would have planned otherwise because the general thinking in that era was that prime time was everything.

From about a quarter to seven to seven o'clock, the switch-board started getting calls from people asking if *Heidi* was going to be showed on time. Then as it got very close to seven, it was mixed between pro-"Heidi" calls and people asking if we were going to stay with the game. [At this point the Jets were winning 32-29 and it was the Raiders' ball with 1:05 to play.] Then once we switched to *Heidi*, all hell broke loose with people scream-ing, "Where's the football game? What happened?" The stories about the calls of complaints haven't been exaggerated. All those phone calls became part of my problem because the sports management people, with whom I was in contact, were trying at around ten to seven to get permission from the presi-dent of NBC [Julian Goodman] to stay with the game. I waited and didn't get a call. I finally called an executive who had two home phone lines, but both were busy. When nobody called me, I went with our original plan.

After I took the game off the air, I heard nothing because our entire switchboard exchange had blown from the phone calls. [At the time, the estimate was 10,000 callers from New York, more than 2,000 from Chicago, and even 1,000 calls from Buf-falo.] And from 6:45 to 7:45 they blew 26 fuses. They'd put one in and it would blow. They'd put another one in and it would blow. So I sat there in the eye of a hurricane. Nobody was get-ting through except the lucky person who happened to call as soon as they got a new fuse in the line.

In those days, there were no satellites, so the game was fed through telephone lines on a big loop between New York and Chicago. There was no monitor in New York where we could watch the game while still showing *Heidi*. So I had no way of knowing what was happening in that last minute and a half. The fact that the game turned out to be as exciting as it did obviously put salt in the wound. People always ask me why I wasn't fired. In fact, I was told the next day that if I had stayed with the game, I would have been fired for defying orders.

The next week, to promote the Jets game, NBC put an ad in the paper where Namath was with somebody dressed up as

"Heidi." It was terrific because instead of hiding, the network used the incident for promotional purposes.

ZIMMERMAN: That wasn't the only thing NBC did. Three weeks later newspapers carried an NBC ad for *Pinocchio*, which would follow a Kansas City-San Diego game. The ad read: "Pinocchio says I'd rather cut off my nose than have them cut off any of today's AFL action. Sports fans can relax. See all the action ... and *Pinocchio*, too (7 P.M.) on NBC!"

CLINE: One long-term impact of the "Heidi game" was sliding the network for long games. We also put in a special phone on a different exchange so people could get through. As a matter of fact, it's still there and it's been called the "Heidi phone" since day one. I'm sure the young folks working at NBC now haven't got a clue as to why it's called that. They're always trying to figure out what H-E-I-D-I means.

The interest in the "Heidi game" is sort of a phenomenon that I'm flabbergasted about at this point. I mean, I wonder if this *Heidi* thing will ever die. It's just got to at some point. Maybe now that it's past 20 years, people will stop asking me about it. At least until the 25th anniversary, when some old-timer will probably call.

The AFL Championship Game

MAYNARD: I don't remember the guys discussing whether or not they'd be satisfied just getting to the Super Bowl. It never really came up. But I remember walking around the locker room at half time of the Oakland game, patting guys on the butt and saying, "This is the game we've got to win. This is the most important game of my life. We've got to win this game to get the honor of going to the Super Bowl. Shoot, the Super Bowl ain't no pressure. You're gonna get the loser's share and if you work a little harder, you're gonna get the winner's share. But the game you've got to win, the pressure game, is the league champion-ship game."

RASMUSSEN: Any time we went into a Raiders game, we knew we were gonna come out of it sore. Guaranteed to get the crap beat out of you. They were a rough, physical team. Dislike isn't the word I'd use for how we felt about them. Downright hatred would be more accurate. One time, I accidentally cut [tackle] Dan Birdwell and he says, "You cut me one more time and I'm going to kill you." And [end] Ben Davidson, he was just the biggest cheap shot artist in the world. So there was no love lost between us.

As a team, I didn't think they were as good as the Colts, but unlike the Colts, they would gamble on defense. The Colts blitzes were very standard blitzes. I mean, you knew what was coming. With those damn Raiders, you never knew what they would try—two linebackers from the same side, drop a lineman back—totally unorthodox crap.

ZIMMERMAN: Wanna know how tough the Raiders played? After the "Heidi game" films came back, Weeb took us down to a little college inn in California and showed us the close-ups on the game. I never saw such ferocity on a football field in my life. I saw stuff I'd never seen before. I saw Dan Birdwell rush Namath, and just after Namath moved, Birdwell put his fist right into Namath's balls as hard as he could. And he just jackknifed him like that. Joe laid on the ground for several minutes, got up and kept playing. I saw Birdwell trying to stand up on Dave Herman's ass, stuff like that. Weeb wanted us to see the films because he was pissed off at how dirty the Raiders were. And we all wrote about it and the club got fined $5,000 for showing us the films.

JIM TURNER: It was an extremely cold day, with those 30-35 mile per hour Shea Stadium winds that would swirl all over the place. I made a 32-yarder in the first quarter to put us up 10-zip, but then I tried a 44-yarder in the second quarter and the wind blew it out. Before the half ended, I hit one from 36 to make it 13-7, so I feel I made some real key ones. We were lucky because we practiced at Shea every day, so I knew the winds.

71

The AFL Championship Game. Fred Biletnikoff scores on a pass from Oakland quarterback Daryle Lamonica. (UPI Photo)

The AFL Championship Game. Jim Turner is kicking one of his three field goals. The Jets won the game 27-23. (UPI/Bettmann Newsphotos)

Knowing our home field gave us an advantage that day. There's a play on an NFL film of the game where Joe comes off the field and Weeb tells him to hit Pete [Lammons] in the corner of the end zone. Well, that particular corner dropped down about three and a half feet from the goal line to the end zone. That was where home plate was for the baseball games and at that end of Shea, the closed one, it really dropped down. You've got to know those nuances when you're the home team.

SAMPLE: A lot of people made a big deal out of the fact that Fred Biletnikoff had such a good day against me [seven catches for 190 yards and one touchdown]. Well, I don't think I played that badly. On that second quarter touchdown he caught off a post-pattern, he was right in front of me. I played that almost as well as I could play it. After he caught the ball, I went to make the tackle and my right foot caught my left heel and it threw me off balance and he jerked away and ran it in.

Weeb benched me for a few plays after that and put in Cornell Gordon. That was the only time I've ever been taken out of a ballgame during my 12 years in pro football. I'll tell you, I was burning sitting on the bench like that. What pissed me off more than the touchdown was that I couldn't go right back in and get even. But I got back in later and Biletnikoff didn't catch any more touchdowns, right?

ZIMMERMAN: The Jets were winning 10-7 in the second quarter when Ben Davidson, who was famous for his handlebar mustache and breaking Namath's jaw the previous year, sacked Namath. Ike Lassiter, the Raiders' 270-pound defensive end, stood over Namath like a gladiator waiting for Nero to give the thumbs-down signal. Lassiter was pointing at Namath and yelling, "We got him, we got him." You could see Namath was hurt. He got up slow and looked very punchy. Earlier in the game, the Raiders had jammed his right thumb and the ring finger on his left hand popped out of joint and was sticking up like a broken board on a picket fence.

HILL: We were coming off the field and I looked at Joe's finger and it was horrible. As soon as we got to the sidelines, the trainer [Jeff Snedeker] yanked it back into place. It must have hurt something terrible.

BABE PARILLI (BACKUP QUARTERBACK): Joe just didn't seem right after the Davidson hit. I said, "Look, if its really bothering you, just come out of the game. I'll be ready. Don't signal to me. Just come on out, so it won't cost us a time out." I watched him closely. He was taking a little longer to set up. His ball wasn't snapping in there as hard. Then, in the third quarter, he completed a 20-yard slant-in to Maynard—I mean he really fired it—and I knew he was okay.

NAMATH (in '69): George Atkinson, their rookie cornerback, intercepted a pass to Don that set up the touchdown putting them up 23-20. I'd tackled him after the interception—one of my rare tackles—on about our four-yard line. I knocked him out of bounds. As he got up, he said, "You sonofabitch, I hate you and I'm gonna kill you." I said, "Hey, man, lighten up. Play the damn game and keep you mouth shut, you know." When we came out after the kickoff, we had the ball on our own 32-yard line and I felt strong. The adrenaline was flowing and I felt confident that we would score.

The Winning Drive

MAYNARD: I was being covered by Atkinson, who I'd beaten pretty bad in the "Heidi game" [10 receptions and 228 yards, a Jets club record] and I was doing pretty well against him again [Maynard had six catches for 188 yards and two touchdowns in this game]. Earlier in the game, after watching the way Atkinson was reacting to my moves, I told Joe, "I've got a long one ...when you need it." Well, we were down 23-20 with about eight minutes left and we needed it. First, Joe hit Sauer on the left side for 10 yards. In the huddle before the next play, Joe said, "We're gonna go for it on this one, so you guys up front hold 'em out just a little longer and be careful."

Namath passes over giant Ben Davidson of the Raiders. (AP Wirephoto)

Namath's pass to Don Maynard erases a 20-23 deficit, ensuring the Jet win. It was Maynard's second touchdown reception. (UPI Photo)

Joe Namath falling on the ball as time runs out. (UPI Photo)

So I run down the right side and Atkinson's running parallel with me to my left. I was a little bit ahead of him, and as I went up for the ball, I was reaching out to the inside at about 10 o'clock. As the ball was about to fall into my hands, the wind—which was always pretty tricky at Shea, especially that day—caught it and I had to turn to my right looking at the ball with my head craned back to keep my eyes on it. All of a sudden, my hands revolved all around, 11, 12 o'clock and I caught it at about one-two o'clock. The direction change caused me to run out of bounds on the six-yard line. If the wind hadn't been there, I would have caught it over my left shoulder and run on in for a touchdown.

NAMATH: Twenty years later that touchdown drive in the championship game is incredibly vivid to me. I can see it, I can feel it, I still get chills talking about it. It wasn't just the last play when we scored the touchdown, it was the three plays in a row. The first one to Sauer seemed like a little insignificant eight-yard out pattern, but it got us a first down right away. When we came to the line of scrimmage, we saw [cornerbacks] Willie Brown and George Atkinson were laid off the receivers seven, eight yards deep, which was something they didn't normally do, so we hit them right away with Sauer.

On second down, I got in the huddle and remembered Don telling me he could get a step on Atkinson if I wanted to go deep. So I called two plays. I said, "Look, if they're laid off again, we'll call this play. If they climb up to the line, I'm gonna check off and I want maximum protection. Don's gonna get a step so be alert for the audible." Well, when we got up to the line, sure enough, they climbed up. I went deep to Don and I can see it as I talk about it. I didn't wind up, but I got a lot on it. I didn't think Don had it. I tried to lay it inside and thought I laid it inside too far. I didn't see him falling back for the ball, and when he got it, man, I was surprised. Although with Don, I know I shouldn't have been. It was one of the greatest catches I've ever seen.

As we were going down the field, words came to me that a fellow had said a few weeks earlier in the old nightclub, Bachelor's III. We called him "Petey the cab driver" and he was a real ardent football fan. Petey once said to me, "Geez, Joe, every time you guys get close, you go into that ball control stuff." He was referring to that stretch where we didn't throw a touchdown pass for six games and were playing conservative, letting Jim Turner kick all those field goals. But before that touchdown play against the Raiders, I heard Petey's words.

When I got back in the huddle, I knew exactly what I was going to do. I figured they'd be expecting Matt Snell to carry the ball on the left side because that play had been so effective. So I called for a fake to Snell, then a little pass out to the left to Bill Mathis which I didn't think they would expect. I was wrong. They had that thing covered like you wouldn't believe. After the fake handoff, I rolled out to my left and Matt blocked the linebacker [Gus Otto] on that side, but he had me contained. Just as I started to pass to Mathis, I saw their safety, Dave Grayson, come up to cover him. Then I looked for Sauer, who had been split out on the left and had gone straight downfield before cutting to the middle, but he was covered. Pete Lammons had cut across from the right side to the left, but they had him covered, too. Five seconds must have gone by and I still had the blocking. The line was just great.

HERMAN: I felt like I was blocking on that play forever.

NAMATH: Finally, I looked for Maynard who had been working purely on instinct. There wasn't a definite time for him to make his break. It wasn't a timing pattern because he was the fourth receiver and his time to come open had to be after I checked the other three. He had started out on the right and just fooled around at the line of scrimmage, acting like he wasn't part of the play. When he saw me in trouble, he darted down the middle. I was gonna throw the ball out of the end zone, but then I saw Don get a step on Atkinson and I knew I could get him the ball. But right before I saw Don, my left leg went out from under me because down at that end the field was in horrendous shape. But I was able to adjust my feet and get in the proper position to throw. I threw that ball as hard as I'd ever thrown a pass. It zipped past Atkinson and Don caught it near the back of the end zone.

MAYNARD: Atkinson was practically shaking hands with me on that play, but Joe just made an unbelievable throw. He led me to the left where I still had to go another two to three yards to make the catch and he made it impossible for Atkinson to get to the ball.

Somebody asked me after the game if I considered myself wide open on those passes. I said, "Well, it all depends on what you call wide open. If you catch a ball and your man misses it by an inch, you might as well say you're wide open."

BIGGS: After we got that touchdown, we were up by four so they needed a touchdown to win. They got down to about our 25-yard line and decided to go for it on a fourth down and I sacked Lamonica. It wasn't just a sack, it was THE sack, the one that guaranteed us going to the Super Bowl.

BAKER: The Raiders got one more series after Verlon's sack and started driving again. They got to about our 25-yard line with a little over two minutes left. Lamonica then throws a swing pass behind [halfback] Charlie Smith, who was my responsibility. I knew it was a lateral so I went after it, but Smith was kind of nonchalant about it. Guess he thought it was just incomplete. I picked it up and ran down the field. It was kind of funny. I would run full speed and Smith would chase me full speed, then I would slow down and turn around to see if they'd blown the play dead and he would slow down and turn around. See, you couldn't advance an incomplete lateral. But earlier in the year there was a similar play on our team and a Patriots linebacker ran it in and they counted it. The referees blew it. So I was pretty upset I couldn't get away with it in the title game.

ZIMMERMAN: It was just another typical Jets-Raiders shootout. I can't remember a low score in a Jets-Raiders game I covered. Namath really had to go balls out in that game. He hit Pete Lammons with a 10-yard pass that Lammons ran in for a touchdown in the third quarter. Lammons said later that he could hear the ball, that the thing whistled when it was coming to him. He said Namath was like a gunner trying to sight. He said he couldn't believe it. See, that's what everybody thought the Jets would be like in the Super Bowl. That it would be a defensive nightmare and everybody would be putting the ball up for grabs. But the Jets switched gears.

NAMATH (in '69): I cried after that championship game. I've only cried after three games in my life. My sophomore year at Alabama, we beat Florida when they missed a field goal in the last minute. I cried after that. And after the Buffalo game when I threw the five interceptions and they ran three of them back for touchdowns with my father there, I cried then. And then the championship game. [Backup cornerback] Cornell Gordon was falling all over me and we were crying together and that was the greatest day, the greatest.

PHILBIN: If there was one game we wanted to win, it was that championship game. The Raiders were the team we wanted to beat. Y'know, to stuff it right in their faces and go to the Super Bowl. And we did it. I remember feeling great that we could do it in front of our fans. I was probably more excited at the end of that game than I ended up feeling at the end of the Super Bowl game. We had a lot of time to savor that victory together before the Super Bowl even had to be played. We celebrated that win so much the Super Bowl was almost anti-climactic.

HERMAN: What made that season so successful was everybody staying healthy. We didn't have any key injuries. None of your winning teams have any significant injuries. And that was crucial to us because we were as thin as thin could be. We didn't play with more than 24-25 guys. We substituted Carl McAdams and Paul Rochester at left tackle and that was it. We had Bob

Talamini replace Sam Walton on the offensive line, but all our other units stayed intact. You don't see that today. Now they change half the unit on almost every play.

BAKE TURNER: One of the perks of winning the championship for me was being able to sing on television. I would pick a guitar and sing country-western tunes in the locker room and a lot of the guys liked it. I was pretty shy about singing in public, but whenever we went to a honky-tonk or someplace on the road, Grantham, Maynard and Turner would always make me get up and sing. Got me over my nervousness about performing in front of people.

Anyway, after we won the Raiders game, Johnny Carson—his show was in New York in those days—came into the locker room and Joe doused him with champagne. I guess he liked it 'cause he invited me, Joe, Maynard and Jim Turner on *The Tonight Show* to sing some songs. Joe didn't sing with us. He just sat on the couch with Ed [McMahon].

The following Sunday, the same group of us went on *The Ed Sullivan Show*. I remember Sullivan asking Joe what kind of music it was we were singing. Sullivan acted like he'd never heard country music before. Guess he never had Johnny Cash or Roy Orbison on "the really big shew."

CHAPTER FOUR

Super Bowl III: The Pre-Game Show

The moment the New York Jets became the champions of the American Football League, they also became one of the most famous underdogs in sports history. Not since some Indians went up against the heavily-favored General Custer at the Little Big Horn was a group of men deemed to have such little chance of success. Despite ranking first in defense and third in offense in the AFL, the Jets were rated by the odds-makers, most notably Jimmy "The Greek" Snyder, as being 17 or more points worse than the National Football League champion Baltimore Colts, their opponents in Super Bowl III.

According to the pundits, the 1968 Colts may have been the best football team ever assembled, maybe even better than the Green Bay Packers' team which had handily won the first two Super Bowls. Coached by 38-year-old Don Shula, already in his sixth year at the helm, Baltimore had compiled an 11-1-2 record in 1967 and a 13-1 mark in '68, becoming only the fourth NFL team to win that many games in a season. The Colts' vaunted defense yielded only 144 points (42 fewer than their closest competitor) and produced three shutouts during the regular season. When they demolished the Cleveland Browns (which had been the only team to beat the Colts that year), 34-0, in the NFL Championship Game, Baltimore's stock rose even higher in the eyes of the pre-Super Bowl prognosticators.

The dominating defensive line was sparked by 6'7", 295-pound sophomore left end Bubba Smith. Next to him were a group of seasoned veterans: 33-year-old All-Pro left tackle Billy Ray Smith, sixth-year right tackle Fred Miller, and 36-year-old right end Ordell Braase, a 6'4", 245-pounder in his 12th year.

At linebacker, 33-year-old Don Shinnick and sixth-year pro Dennis Gaubatz were solid, but had become overshadowed by 6'2", 232-pound left linebacker Mike Curtis, already an All-Pro at 24. Curtis, a savage hitter, was known as "the animal." Curtis's lining up on the same side as "Kill, Bubba, Kill" Smith discouraged many running backs from scampering to the left.

The Colts' secondary had intercepted 22 passes during the season and featured Lenny Lyles and Bobby Boyd at corner-back, veterans with 20 years experience between them. Sixth-year man Jerry Logan was the strong safety and sophomore All-Pro Rick Volk was the freelancer at the other safety spot. Lou Michaels (Jets' defensive coach Walt Michaels' younger brother), who finished third in the NFL in scoring with 102 points, was the field-goal specialist. The kickoff-return specialist was Preston Pearson, who led the league with a 35.1 return average—fourth highest in NFL history—and had returned kicks of 96 and 102 yards for touchdowns.

Prior to the season, few would have believed the Colts could score 402 points, let alone get to the Super Bowl, with Johnny Unitas sitting on the bench all year instead of standing behind the center. But when a chronic right elbow injury sidelined the 35-year-old living legend, veteran backup Earl Morrall stepped in and had the proverbial "Cinderella" season. The 12-year journeyman had played for four other teams before joining the Colts during training camp. All he did in 1968 was lead the NFL in passing and touchdown passes (26), finish third in average yards per pass (9.18) and completion percentage (57.4), and earn the league's Player of the Year honors. So going into the Super Bowl, the Colts had to feel extremely confident with Morrall as the starter and a future Hall of Famer ready if he faltered.

Morrall certainly felt secure behind a veteran offensive line consisting of All-Pro Bob Vogel and Sam Ball at the tackles, guards Glenn Ressler and Dan Sullivan and center Bill Curry. The running backs, Tom Matte and Jerry Hill, weren't game-breakers, but were versatile, dependable, and followed their blocking well. In flanker Willie Richardson and split end Jimmy Orr, the Colts had one of the best wide-out tandems in football. But the impact player of the Baltimore offense was 6′2″, 225-pound tight end John Mackey. The six-year veteran (who had been a former Jets draft choice) was one of football's most dangerous open-field receivers and had led the Colts with 45 receptions at 14.3 yards per catch. Mackey, who was also a devastating blocker, was the Colts player the Jets most feared.

So impressive was this Baltimore team in the eyes of the journalists covering Super Bowl III, that in a pool of 55 sportswriters (credentials were given to 834 writers, photographers and members of the electronic media, over 600 more than were in Vietnam), 49 predicted a Colts victory. *Sports Illustrated*'s top football writer Tex Maule picked the Colts to win 43-0.

The Jets' players were among the few who scoffed at the point-spread and the predictions. And they weren't just spouting the usual cliches underdogs use about being "confident." They carefully analyzed the Colts' game films and saw that their strengths matched-up well with Baltimore's weaknesses, especially their offense versus the Colts' defense. Despite all the talk about NFL "dominance" and Baltimore "invincibility" that was swirling around them, the Jets felt their top AFL competition— the Oakland Raiders and Kansas City Chiefs—was on par with the best of the NFL.

When the Jets weren't giving rave reviews to the Baltimore game films, they were soaking up the sun under the relaxed "it's-just-like-any-other-game" atmosphere created by coach Weeb Ewbank. In fact, things were so relaxed and the team was so confident, they spent part of their first day in Florida complaining about having to pay for their wives' trip and trying to substantiate a rumor that they would be getting watches instead of AFL championship rings.

83

Super Bowl preview. Opposing quarterbacks: Earl Morrall of the NFL Championship Baltimore Colts, and Joe Namath of the underdog New York Jets. (AP Wirephotos)

But most of the pre-game attention focused on Namath, who was turning Super Bowl hype into an art form just by saying what he thought. The most creative publicist in the world couldn't have conjured up the kind of headline-grabbing itinerary that Namath created with his daily words and actions.

On the Thursday, January 2nd flight to Miami after the AFL title game, Namath declared that there were five AFL quarterbacks better than Earl Morrall and that Morrall would rank no higher than third-string behind Babe Parilli on the Jets. On Sunday the 5th, Namath engaged in a war of words with Colts kicker Lou Michaels in a Miami restaurant. The next morning, Namath missed a scheduled team-photo session. And on Thursday the 9th, he made one of the most famous statements in sports history, when at the Miami Touchdown Club banquet, he boldly guaranteed a Jets victory.

Joe Namath was making Super Bowl III a legendary game even before the two teams played a single down.

The Spread

JIMMY "THE GREEK" SNYDER (two weeks before the Super Bowl): The number is 17. The Colts over the Jets by 17. The AFL is improving, but the Jets have a tiger by the tail. The Colts have the greatest defensive team in football history, better than the Packers. In coming up with a 17-point differential, I give the Colts 12 points on defense alone—a four-point edge to their front four, four to the linebackers, and four to their defensive backs. They're the first team I've ever given more than three points in any defensive category.

The quarterbacks are even. I rate Namath a five-point quarterback. He and Sonny Jurgensen are the only ones I rate that high. Earl Morrall is worth three points, but having Johnny Unitas behind him makes the quarterbacking even. The receivers are even and so are the field-goal kickers. Jim Turner had a great year, but Lou Michaels has more experience. In overall team speed, they're even, but I give the Colts a two-point edge in the running game. Tom Matte is fantastic and Jerry Hill is a great run-blocker. If the Colts can hold Leroy Kelly of Cleveland to 28 yards in 13 carries in the championship game, then Matt Snell and Emerson Boozer won't be able to do much. Without a running game, the pass rush will be hurrying Namath.

So that's 14 points, plus three for intangibles like the NFL mystique and Don Shula's coaching. Until they blanked the Browns, I was figuring on the Colts by about 12, but now it's got to be 17.

ZIMMERMAN: Somebody asked [Green Bay Packers coach] Vince Lombardi what he thought about the Jets being 17-point underdogs and Lombardi said, "Well, I'm not suppose to talk about point spreads or gambling, but 17 points is too much to give a quarterback like Namath."

SNELL: That point-spread was embarrassing. Even if you wanted to say the AFL was a junior league, there's no way we could be 17-point underdogs. I guess those guys in Las Vegas know what they're doing most of the time, but I don't know where they got that spread from. They probably based it on the first two games, except now they wouldn't have Green Bay on the other side of the ball. But there was no way we could be 17 points worse than Baltimore. They had to score more than two touchdowns than us before somebody could win a bet on them? Come on, give me a break.

As far as those matchups were concerned, I couldn't believe guys like Jimmy the Greek could say that Matte and Hill were better than me and Boozer. If we weren't better than those guys, we were in sad shape. It really made me mad. In our hotel room, I said to Emerson, "Booz, for the first time in my life, I'm going to be looking for people to run into. I'm going to be looking to punish people."

HUDSON: I don't think many of the guys knew what the point-spread was. We knew we were underdogs, but hell, as far as a bettin' line goes, nobody paid attention to it and nobody really cared on our team.

GEORGE SAUER: What I don't understand is why the Dallas Cowboys [who were 12-2 and won a NFL divisional title in 1968] could be rated so much better than the best AFL teams when they started in 1960 just as we did.

GRANTHAM: That point-spread was just another example of how nobody took us seriously. I mean nobody. I couldn't understand why they didn't think we were up to the caliber of NFL teams. In New York at that time, the Giants got better treatment, even though we were a better team, because they were "older and established." You know, a Jet player would go out to a speaking engagement and be paid 100 bucks to sit on the same dais with a Giant player who was getting $500 for the same amount of time and effort.

NAMATH (comments made prior to the Super Bowl): I didn't know we were that bad a football team. If we were allowed to bet, I'd bet a hundred thousand on us on this one. It's going to be a challenge for us, but it's going to be a challenge for them, too. I might sound like I'm boasting and bragging, and I am. When the Colts lost to the Browns at mid-season, they didn't get beat by any powerhouse. I'm not going to take what I read about their defense. I'm going to go with what the one-eyed monster [the film projector] shows me.

You put Babe Parilli with Baltimore instead of Morrall and Baltimore might've been better. Babe throws better than Morrall. I might be prejudiced about that, because Babe is with us. But I believe it. If you put any pro quarterback on our team, only a few wouldn't be third-string. That's my opinion. I don't care how people value my opinion, but I value it very highly, especially when I'm talking about football. And as for all that talk about the NFL being a better league, well, there are more teams in the NFL, so they should have more good teams. But you put their good teams and our good teams together, or their bad teams and our bad teams together, it's 50-50, flip a coin. And we've got better quarterbacks in our league—John Hadl

[San Diego], Len Dawson [Kansas City], Daryle Lamonica, my-self, Bob Griese [Miami].

I read where some NFL guy joked about Lamonica and me throwing nearly 100 passes last Sunday. And we threw 97, but what's so terrible about that? How many NFL teams have a quarterback who could complete as many passes to their wide receivers as we do? In our league, we throw much more to our wide receivers than they do to theirs. I completed 49 percent of my passes this season, but I could've completed 80 percent if I dropped the ball off to my backs like they do in the NFL.

And I've got the best receivers. George Sauer has the best moves, nobody can cover him one-on-one, and Don Maynard is the smartest. And when a quarterback has wide receivers that good, he *should* throw to them.

Miami Vices

ZIMMERMAN: During the first week before the game, the point-spread went up to as much as 19 and a half points because of how crazy things were with the Jets. They had their families down there and the hotel [the Galt Ocean Mile in Ft. Lauder-dale] was a zoo, wives chasing kids around, wives bugging the husbands all the time, the players rebelling about how much the team was going to pay for rings and who would pay for flying the wives down. Then Namath gets into a verbal brawl with Lou Michaels in a bar and misses picture day the next day because he's too hungover to go. I mean they looked like the biggest losers you ever saw. I had a writer friend who had bet the Jets with the 17 points and with a week to go before the game, he was biting his finger nails off. He says the team is gonna get killed. So he calls his bookie and bets the Colts giving 19 and a half points. If the Colts win by 18, he loses both bets.

JIM TURNER: After we arrived in Florida, we had a meeting with Weeb because we heard the team was going to make us pay for our wives' expenses, that we might get watches instead of rings for winning the AFL championship, stuff like that. There were always things like that going on with the team. It probably made the players feel closer together. It might sound like we were pretty cocky; worrying about rings before the biggest game of lives. But we were worried about being taken care of. We'd heard that with the Packers, Vince Lombardi had thrown a big party, flown all the wives in, bought them all mink coats. And here we were going to have to pay for one half of our rooms for our own wives, which ended being eight to 10 bucks a day. I think all of us felt cheated. It wasn't so much the money. We just wanted to be treated properly.

BIGGS: I remember Jim Turner being really upset about the team not wanting to pay for the wives. He told Weeb, "You make us pay for our wives, you can get yourself another kicker."

GRANTHAM: Yeah, we worried about our rings. We felt like we were going to win the ballgame and we wanted to make sure that the proper attention was given to those rings.

But that stuff wasn't going to affect us on the field. We took the attitude that we were just glad to be there. Weeb wanted us to prepare just like it was another football game at the end of the season. He didn't put any pressure on us to win or lose. We didn't read a lot about the game in the papers. I didn't even know, until somebody pointed it out to me the night before the game, that we were 18-point underdogs.

We were so relaxed that we spent three or four nights before the game out by the pool laughing and cutting up. We were trying to throw our business manager John Free into the pool while he had all our per diem checks in his pockets.

DOCKERY: A bunch of us chartered two yachts and went deep sea fishing one day. I was on one with Winston Hill and his wife, Carolyn. Before we set out, each of us put up $10 and the boat catching the biggest fish would get the pot. Anyway, we're sailing along and all of a sudden Winston hooks a big one. It turned out to be a hammerhead shark. That thing must have been seven feet long. Winston finally won the battle, but it was too heavy to bring on board. When the other boat saw our catch, Matt Snell yelled, "No good. It has to be edible."

SAMPLE: Lenny Lyles and I had been roommates on the Colts, and on the Wednesday night before the game, he asked me if I wanted to hang out with him and Willie Richardson. I told him I couldn't go out with Richardson because I'd be covering him on Sunday. I told Lenny that if we go out and he buys me a beer and we sit around talking all night, I really might like him and I didn't want that to happen before a big game.

ELLIOTT: The atmosphere was so relaxed that week. It was the same game as it is today, but it wasn't built up as much. One night we went to the dog races, another night to a Jai Alai game, another night to a movie—I think we saw John Wayne in *Hellfighters* about Red Adair. I remember everyday after practice we went to this place that had the best hot dogs in the world. Weenie in a bun with chopped onions and chili powder. I still eat my hot dogs like that today.

We didn't have a curfew until late the second week, but by that time we were so tired we needed it. We couldn't go out even if we wanted to. It wasn't from partying, but from going out all the time. There was something to do every day. Weeb said, "Just don't get into trouble. Go out, have a good time, but keep your nose clean. Don't do anything to hurt yourself or hurt the team." I think that was a good move. If we'd had to be in our rooms by 11:00 every night and all we had to think about was the game, we might have been so strung out by the day of the game we couldn't have done anything.

HUDSON: It would be unheard of today, but we had guys missing practice before the Super Bowl. We got down to Miami on a Thursday and before our curfew started on the Tuesday before the game we had guys who'd come in four, five, six, seven in the morning. The "no curfew" was voted on at a team meeting with Weeb, who was big on voting. By the time he got through with the vote, everybody had voted no curfew and he really had no alternative. We weren't gonna make curfew anyway and Weeb was smart enough to realize that.

JOHNSON: That vote we had about bed check was really funny. Weeb says, "Okay, how many guys think we should be in bed by 10:00?" Nobody raised their hands. "How many think we should be in bed by 11:00?" Nobody raised their hands. It got up past midnight, so Weeb says, "Well, I guess, damn it, y'all don't want a bed check." We said, "That sounds like a winner, Weeb. Let's not have a bed check." We were all grown men. We knew we'd come down there to win. If people wanted to go to bed early, fine. If other guys want to go out and raise hell and get out of shape and prevent us from being the first AFL team to win the Super Bowl, it would be our fault. So the first few nights a lot of guys stayed out late, but you could see as it got closer to the game, the more dedicated everybody would get. You would really see it in practice. We were working harder. In fact, the coaches would have to run us off the field because we were out there in the heat too long.

The Namath-Michaels "Brawl"

HUDSON: We didn't have a curfew that Sunday night when Joe and I went to Jimmy Fazio's restaurant and had our little confrontation with Lou Michaels. Boy, did the media blow that thing out of proportion. They made it sound like a big brawl. It never got that far. What happened was Michaels and [Colts guard] Dan Sullivan had snuck out of curfew and came into the restaurant about three or four in the morning. Joe knew Lou— his older brother Frank had roomed with Lou at Kentucky— and they started out going back and forth with "We're gonna kick the shit out of you" and stuff like that. Then they got into who was the best Catholic. Just a couple of drunks arguing about religion and that kind of junk. Anyway, it was getting pretty heated for a while. I said to Sullivan, "Damn, man, we've got to calm this down before we get into a fight in here." They might have come to blows, but I know I wasn't wantin' to get into blows. Joe and I were about 205 pounds and they were about 250. But I wasn't worried about Joe getting hurt, I was worried about me, heh, heh. Joe ended up picking up the check and driving them back to their hotel.

LOU MICHAELS (COLTS PLACE KICKER): I know I didn't want to cause any trouble. I knew that Walt would be mad if I knocked the head off the only guy who had any chance at all of beating us. Namath struck people as being cocky, but I came away thinking that he was a real gentleman. The only reason I showed any resentment to begin with was because he said the Jets were going whip us and kick the hell out of us. But I found he was a pretty good guy.

DON SHULA (COLTS HEAD COACH): Our football team was conscious of everything that was written. We had a pretty good laugh out of the thing that happened between Lou Michaels and Namath. The guys were telling Lou that Namath bought him off by picking up the dinner check. Actually, Joe was the 837th guy that Michaels has threatened to deck. If Lou had punched Joe, it would have been just the 37th guy that he actually hit.

ZIMMERMAN: The Monday morning after the Namath-Michaels incident, Joe, Snell and Boozer [the running backs overslept] didn't show up for photo day and the situation was a little tense. But Weeb, who was a wily old dog, tried to get us off the subject. He starts telling the writers, "You know, sometimes the team gets too tight and I have to loosen them up and I'll even tell a dirty joke." Somebody said, "Give us an example." Weeb saw a waitress and said, "Little lady, would you please leave the room." So he starts telling the joke. "A lady walks into a doctor's office and says she's got a hormone imbalance. The doctor says, "What do you mean?" She says, "I've got hair on my chest." The doctor says, "Take off your blouse and let's see." So she takes off the blouse and sure enough there's hair on her chest. The doctor asks her how far down it goes. She says, "Right down to my balls."

92

There's another funny story about picture day. I was working on an article on the Michaels brothers. So first I got Walt to talk about his family and everything. Then I went down the coast to the Colts camp to talk to Louie. The atmosphere at the Super Bowl was a lot looser than it is now. My wife was with me and there were kids on the field. Anyway, Lou starts telling me about their father and how the guy died before he could really see them play and how happy he'd be now. And all of a sudden he starts crying. The tears are coming down and people are backing off, my wife is getting nervous. He's really sobbing. I say, "Thanks a lot, Lou" and start to leave and he says, "Wait a minute," and pulls me back and starts telling me more. It was an incredibly emotional scene.

Then we walk away and I see Jimmy Orr standing on the sideline sort of cackling and I said, "Did you see that?" and he says, "Yeah." I said, "He was crying." He said, "You'd be crying too if you were drinking vodka until five in the morning."

The Namath Pool Conference

LARRY MERCHANT (*New York Post* column of Friday, January 10, 1969): Having been tucked into bed at midnight, Joe Namath came out Thursday morning for the rays. The phenomenon of Joe Namath and Joe Namath Week, which is roaring to its climax or anti-climax in the Super Bowl on Sunday, was distilled into a half-hour show of pure Broadway Joe.

Namath sat down in a beach chair by the pool and before you could say "26-x, blue right slot double, 11 on two," he was in the middle of a huddle. His linemen were reporters, his ends were kids, his backs were middle-aged ladies.

The reporters were uninvited and not really welcome visitors because they were foreign correspondents whom Namath had expressed a desire not to see. He did not wish to explain his most recent caper to them, the Lou Michaels thing, because he knew from experience that explanations would merely fan dying embers. Also, you don't repeat a joke.

Namath senses that strange reporters are from NFL cities and probably reflect the uptight establishment view of his craziness. He is a perfect litmus test for the generation gap, as Muhammad Ali was even in his pro-political and religious maverick stage, as just plain Cassius Clay. It is said that several dozen reporters will dive out of the Orange Bowl press box if Namath does to the Colts what Ali did to Sonny Liston here. This would be a symbolic act for many of the 75 or 100 million people who watch the game would be similarly aggrieved. Mrs. Randy Beverly, wife of the Jet cornerback, almost got into a fight with a grocery man the other day when he learned her husband was a teammate of Joe Namath and therefore wishes him the worst. America today roots for the overdog.

And, of course, Namath has refused to be intimidated by the Super Bowl scene. He has risen to the occasion simply by staying in character....Here he was before many of them, at pool side, on the beach chair. "This wasn't the way I had it planned," he said with a grin, and he proceeded to disarm them by making it all seem perfectly harmless, as it was....

He answered the questions with candor and tact while reading his mail and never offending the questioner, while kibbitzing with kids and flirting with the middle-aged ladies who were in swoons over his blue eyes and dimples....It was a virtuoso performance....Super ability and charm are a deadly combination ...Joe Namath isn't the only one in the Super Bowl game. It just seems that way.

Thursday Knee-Drainings

DAVE ANDERSON (*The New York Times* columnist, from his 1969 book *Countdown to Super Bowl*): Joe Namath and Matt Snell were in the trainer's room. "You first, Matt," said Dr. James Nicholas, "because we'll be working on Joe quite a while."

Stoically, the fullback sat on the rubbing table as the doctor prepared to aspirate his right knee. It had required cartilage surgery early in the 1967 season. "All right," the fullback said as the doctor approached with the needle, "do what you have to do."

About three ounces of the beer-colored fluid appeared in the black-trimmed plastic syringe. "That's the most you've ever had," the doctor said. "You must be really running hard in the practices."

Now it was the quarterback's turn. On a nearby tray, the needles and syringes had been readied. In about 72 hours, Joe Namath would be on the field in the Super Bowl game, his success depending on how he was able to maneuver on his crippled knees. At present, the doctor was preparing to minimize the pain in those knees.

"Five of them," Namath said, staring at the syringes. "That's a record."

Sitting halfway down the rubbing table, Namath held his legs flat in front of him. His arms behind him, a towel across his middle, the quarterback tightened as the doctor approached his left knee. That was the one with the inflamed tendon. In the syringe was Novocaine and the doctor inserted the thin one-inch-long needle below the kneecap. When the Novocaine disappeared, the doctor unscrewed the empty syringe, but left the needle protruding.

"No need to stick you with two needles, I'm just changing the syringe," the doctor said, smiling. "I'm not a sadist."

"Hudson should hear you say that because he thinks you are."

The doctor picked up another syringe with a colorless liquid in it.

"Not yet," the quarterback said. "Give the Novocaine time to work."

"Stop moaning," the doctor said, still smiling, "Diabetics do this every day."

In the new syringe was 25 milligrams of Prednisone, which would relieve the pain in the inflamed tendon for several days. When it vanished into the knee, the doctor withdrew the needle.

"Now we'll tap the right one again," the doctor said.

"Not we, you," Namath said. "Don't give me that we."

As on the previous Saturday, about two ounces of fluid were obtained from the right knee through the three-inch needle.

"Now the left knee again," the doctor said.

This time the needle pierced the skin near the back of the outside of the knee. First the Novocaine. Then the change of syringe. Then another 25 milligrams of Prednisone to shrink the inflammation in the bursal sac.

"Look at them," Namath said, laughing at the needles and syringes that had been tossed in the wastebasket. "Will you look at all those needles."

As the quarterback limped away, the doctor gave him a bottle with red pills—Butazolidin—to decrease the pain in his left knee.

Joe's "Guarantee" of Victory

NAMATH (excerpts from speech after receiving Outstanding Pro Football Player of the Year Award for 1968 at Miami Touchdown Club Banquet, Thursday, January 9, 1969): "This isn't an award for me...this should be a most valuable player award for the entire team. You can be the greatest athlete in the world, but if you don't win those football games, it doesn't mean anything. And we're going to win Sunday, I'll guarantee you....

"Everybody around the Colts is annoyed because I said that Earl Morrall wasn't as good as Daryle Lamonica of the Oakland Raiders, but those are my feelings, and I think I'm entitled to them, just as reporters are entitled to theirs. And, speaking of reporters, I read where one wrote that our defense can't compare with the Colts'. Anybody who knows anything about football knows that we have five guys on defense alone better than them....

"And another thing I want to talk about is hair. Mustaches, beards. They're supposed to create a bad image, but who tells the children that it's a bad image—the parents. I shaved off my mustache because I felt like shaving it off, just like I felt like growing it....

"And about the point-spread, somebody told me it's 19 now. Well, coming down on the plane, it was 17 and Paul Rochester, one of our defensive tackles, said he'd rather be a 17-point underdog than a 19-point favorite, because we were a 19-point favorite twice during the season, and we lost, to Buffalo and Denver, and the Colts should keep that in mind."

NAMATH (20 years after making "guarantee"): After my saying "I guarantee we're gonna win," a lot of the information out of Ft. Lauderdale and Miami had to do with that and it did kind of interrupt the tunnel vision we needed for the game. The statement wasn't planned. There wasn't a motive behind it. It was just something that needed to be said and was a spur of moment thing triggered by a loudmouth Colts fan at that Miami dinner.

When I look back at that period now, I realize that not only was I a very confident young man, I was also very angry, actually. It was more or less anger and frustration stemming from how everybody was putting the team and the league down that led me to make that "guarantee." I mean, you tell any group of men, who have worked for a whole season to get to a championship game, that they're two touchdown underdogs and it has to irritate the people you're putting down."

SCHMITT: On that Friday morning when Joe's "guarantee" story broke, my wife and I were having breakfast and Joe was at the next table looking, well, pretty tired. You know what I mean? Anyway, Weeb comes up to us waving this newspaper that says, "Namath Guarantees Win." I swear to God, Weeb's got tears in his eyes. He says, "Joe, did you see this paper?" Joe didn't respond because he could hardly see anything that morning. Weeb says, "Joe, did you really say that, Joe." And Joe says, "Yeah, coach." And Weeb says, "Ah, Joe, Joe, you know what they're gonna do. They're gonna put that on the locker room wall. Those Colts are gonna want to kill us." And Joe says, "Well, coach, you've been telling us for the last two weeks that we're gonna win, right? I just let the rest of the people know what you've been thinking. Coach, don't you think we're gonna win?""

Weeb says, "Well, of course I do." And Joe just continued eating his breakfast.

I'll tell you, that guarantee was probably one of the greatest things Joe could have done because the Colts were really pissed off. They wanted to kill Namath and kill us. They wanted to eat us alive and that had to throw them off their game.

EWBANK: When we got down to Florida, I told the players not to pay any attention to what I might say to the writers because if I could say some things that might make the point-spread go up to 21, I would do it. I told them to just believe in what we had in our game plan. Then on that Friday morning, someone asked me what I thought about what Joe had said the night before. I didn't know what he had said because I hadn't read the paper. When I heard Joe had guaranteed it, I coulda just shot him. Of course, I told the press I was all for what Joe said, but I really could have killed him. I didn't want to get the Colts riled up. When I said something to Joe about it, his attitude was that if Shula had to use something like that to get this team ready, then hell, we're going to beat them anyway.

BAKER: I can still remember having breakfast and reading the article about Joe guaranteeing the win and thinking to myself, "This guy is crazy." At first I felt he had to have been in a situation where he didn't know what he was saying. How can you guarantee that? Because I didn't feel we knew that much about the Colts. I think Joe's statement made me look at their films in a different light. I thought maybe I'd been missing something. If the leader of the offense felt so strongly about it, you had to reassess the situation.

LAMMONS: You know, we were down there in pretty hostile territory. It was all NFL and Joe was what the writers focused on for the AFL side. Joe was the only guy they wanted to talk to from our team and with the whiskey going in there a little faster, Joe just decided he'd tell 'em what he thought about the whole deal.

But at the beginning of the week, when he said there were a lot better quarterbacks in the AFL than Earl Morrall and that Morrall would be third-string on the Jets, he wasn't belittling anybody. Joe wouldn't do that. Hell, Morrall was second string everywhere until people got hurt. Then he replaces Unitas and wins everything and all of a sudden he's a savior. He did what needed to be done. I'll say that for him.

But when Joe guaranteed the victory, the papers left out a lot of other stuff he said, like explaining in detail why he felt we would win the game. They didn't print that stuff. When we read the papers the next day, it wasn't a big deal to us. If anybody was upset about it, it was probably the guys on the defense.

HERMAN: Joe had some pretty good competition from the press in the "arrogant quote" department. While we were playing Oakland for the title, in the press box at Cleveland for the Colts game was Tex Maule, who was the football writer for *Sports Illustrated*. After he saw us beat Oakland, I guess on the press box television, you know what his quote was? "All right, now let's go watch some real football." So while Joe was saying all that stuff, here was a guy thought to be an expert, who had the eyes of people from every sport from east coast to west coast reading *Sports Illustrated*—and you know how the written word tends to become the bible to a lot of people—getting everybody to say, "Who is this loudmouth guy on the New York Jets?"

The Colts Speak

DON SHULA: I don't know how Namath can rap Earl. After all, Earl's number one in the NFL. He's thrown all those touchdown passes. He's thrown for a great percentage without using dinky flare passes. And he's been voted the Player of the Year in our league. Earl has had a great year for us and we're proud of him. Anyone who doesn't give him the credit he deserves is wrong. But I guess Namath can say whatever the hell he wants.

BILLY RAY SMITH (DEFENSIVE TACKLE): Namath talks too much. When it comes to throwing the football, I have to put him in there with the best I've ever seen. He can throw a ball in a teacup from 50 yards. But he should keep his mouth shut. He'll keep his teeth a lot longer. There's nothing I like to hit more than quarterbacks and when you get a mouthy one, it makes it that much better.

You know, he hasn't seen defenses like ours in the AFL. Our defenses are as complicated as some teams' offenses. We have 20 variations in our blitzes and five or six alignments up front. That lets us do a lot of things. I think reading our defenses will be a new experience for that man.

BUBBA SMITH (DEFENSIVE END, quoted before Super Bowl): I have a bundle of respect for Joe Namath; he's a damned good quarterback, an exceptional quarterback. But a football player who's real good doesn't have to talk. The Green Bay Packers were real champions. They never talked. They never had to. This is the way I visualize all champions—solemn, dignified, humble.

My father coached me at Charlton Pollard High School in Beaumont, Texas, and he taught me to be humble off the field. Inside, I've got to feel I'm the best, but if I tell you that I'm be best, then I'm a fool.

BUBBA SMITH (quoted 20 years after Super Bowl): I'd heard that Namath was guaranteeing a win. But what else can you say when you're 17-18-point underdogs. If they lose, then people would say, "Oh, Joe's just talking out of his head." If they win, then he's a miracle worker. Nobody on our team took what Joe was saying seriously. It never dawned on us that the game could ever be close. The point-spread didn't effect us. We knew if we played them 10 times we'd beat them every time. It's not that we didn't think they were a good team. We knew they had the good receivers and with Joe's quick release we would have to clamp down on them. But I didn't think they had the defensive people to beat us and I didn't think they could compete with any team in our division.

ALEX HAWKINS (BACKUP WIDE RECEIVER): We never recognized the AFL, never watched their games. I never even saw Joe Namath throw until warmups before the Super Bowl. We laughed at their defense because we honestly thought we could score 40 or 50 points against them.

BOBBY BOYD (DEFENSIVE BACK): In the AFL, they play more of a bump-and-run technique. They line up on a guy's nose and try to jam him before he gets out. I don't see the advantage of it. You might do that on the goal line, where there isn't much room to break out. I prefer to sit back and read the receiver, the quarterback and the flare control.

BILL CURRY (CENTER): The whole NFL thing was riding on us. We were gonna be the greatest team in history.

DON SHULA: When we studied film on the Jets, we felt we'd be able to control both lines of scrimmage. Sure, we felt confident of victory. You don't think any other way before any game. I told the team, "Everything we've accomplished all year is riding on this game. We can't wait for the Jets to lose it. We've got to go out and win it ourselves."

The One-Eyed Monster

LAMMONS: On the Tuesday before the game, we all got together to watch the Colts game films. The offense watched their defense and vice-versa. After a few hours we took a break, and while everyone was stretching out, I said to Clive Rush and Joe and the rest of the guys, "Damn, we watch any more of these films, we're gonna get overconfident." Now, it's become kind of a famous line, but then some of the guys laughed and some had kind of a blank look. I think they all realized the same thing; that we could beat those guys. Sometimes I feel like I'm remembered more for that one quote more than I am as a player. At least I gave Joe a little competition. Maybe I even gave him the idea to guarantee the win, heh, heh.

101

JIM TURNER: When Pete made that comment, it wasn't one of those weird, cocky statements where the guy was just being a wise-ass. He was just saying, I think, what everybody felt. After watching the films we believed that their weaknesses—and as good as they were they had some weaknesses—fed our strengths. They had an aging right side—Ordell Braase [36] at right tackle, John Shinnick [33] at right linebacker, and Lenny Lyles [32] at right cornerback—and we felt that whole side was weak. And since we ran to our left or their right, it was perfect for our game plan.

LAMMONS: Let me put it this way: I don't think we were inferior to the Colts and nobody on the team felt inferior. You know, in 1966, I was in the running for the Rookie of the Year and doing a lot of interviews. In one of the interviews—and I remember this very distinctly—someone asked me, "What do you feel like coming to the AFL, do you feel inferior to an NFL tight end?" I gave him a blank look and said, "I don't understand what you're saying here." And so he repeated the question and I said, "Look, when I played at the University of Texas, which is a pretty prestigious football team, we beat some pretty good teams; in fact, we beat Namath and Alabama in the Orange Bowl. If some of those guys we beat go to the NFL and I go to the AFL, does that make them better than me?" He didn't know how the hell to answer me. I said, "So I don't think I'm inferior because I came to the AFL."

SAMPLE: We weren't intimidated by the Colts record or the fact that they beat Cleveland 34-0 in their title game. We watched that game on film and Cleveland looked like a taxi-squad team.

HUDSON: Joe and I spent a lot of time watching films of the Colts games and Joe was analyzing their defense, watching how their safeties moved on particular patterns. He would get real excited whenever he saw something important and run the film over and over. He'd say, "Did you see that, Jim? Did you see the way that safety moved to the inside? Look at the way the Rams ran that play right at the Colts' strength. We'll break those outside receivers to the inside on slants. Hey, see that receiver? He didn't even turn around to help the quarterback. Our receivers turn around." Joe got pretty confident watching those films.

NAMATH (from his 1969 book *I Can't Wait Until Tomorrow 'Cause I Get Better Looking Everyday*): I'll tell you, I enjoyed watching the Colts game films as much as a good Lee Marvin movie. Some people were saying that the Jets'd be scared of the Colts defense. Scared, hell—the only thing that scared me was that they might change their defense.

What I liked best was the Baltimore safety blitz. Lots of times, just before the snap or on the snap, they moved their two safeties, Rick Volk and Jerry Logan, up to fill in the gaps between the linebackers. Sometimes, one safety would blitz—shoot through and try to get the quarterback—and, sometimes, the other one would blitz. No matter who blitzed, they had to leave part of the middle open. I knew I could hit my wide receivers slanting in.

The more I saw of the Baltimore movies, the better I felt. Cleveland and Minnesota and Los Angeles were just plain dumb against the blitz. The Browns kept trying to run through the packed Baltimore line. The Rams used some quick sideline patterns that didn't disrupt the blitz at all. The Vikings didn't do a damn thing to throw the Colts' defense off balance; as far as I could tell, they never varied their count, never took a real long count or a real quick count to break the rhythm of the Colts.

I just prayed the Colts would blitz and if they did, I figured they were dead. Our backs were great at picking up a blitz and our receivers could smell a blitz a mile away.

Anybody who'd ever played in the AFL would tell you not to blitz the New York Jets. I'd been telling people all year that the AFL had caught up to the NFL and people kept telling me I was wrong. Well, I *was* wrong. We'd already passed them in a lot of things.

ZIMMERMAN: Like a lot of people, the Colts had a hard time

believing that Namath was one of football's most intelligent and fundamentally sound quarterbacks. Johnny Unitas, for instance, said that Namath had never seen a defense like the one the Colts were going to throw at him. But Namath didn't look at the Colts in terms of personalities—Mike "The Animal" Curtis, the linebacker who hates everybody; and Billy Ray Smith, who could jump over blockers to get to a quarterback; and the mountainous Bubba Smith, who responded to those "Kill, Bubba, kill!" roars like a Ferrari responds to high octane gas.

What Namath saw, watching the projector, was a little set of moving X's and O's, playing a rotating strong side zone defense. He knew that he could snap the ball into the creases of such a defense because he'd done it before. And he had been dumped for losses only 15 times during the season, less than any other starting quarterback in football, so he wasn't worried about his offensive line breaking down. He was a student, and if there was any trepidation about that final exam, he kept it to himself.

GRANTHAM: When we watched the game films, we noticed that they were winning on a lot of turnovers. They were winning on a lot of big defensive plays. And we knew that our offense wasn't going to give them the big plays; fumbles and interceptions and all that stuff.

So long as our offense played them solid, then we felt our defense could contain them. We didn't see where they had a concentrated running game other than Tom Matte and, you know, it's hard for one man to carry the football down the field constantly. We just couldn't really see that they had the real tough ingredients that it would take to shove the football down some team's throat. And if you stopped their running game, they didn't have anywhere to go except John Mackey, in our opinion.

ELLIOTT: Since we had a relatively small defensive line—nobody expect Biggs was over 245—our main plan was to keep the offensive line off our linebackers and let our linebackers make all the penetration. Our game plan after watching the Colts films was that as soon as the ball was snapped, we'd go straight ahead. We ran an odd-man line quite a bit and Baltimore had never see that before. They were used to big defensive tackles lining up over the outside shoulder of the guards and the ends lining up on the outside shoulder of the tackles. With that alignment, your middle linebacker is standing there where a center can take a clean shot at him. We were gonna shoot the gaps. I would line up head-up on the center, or one time I would loop between the guard and the center on one side and they'd never know which way I was going. That would freeze the center and guard for a half a count and would give our middle linebacker, Al Atkinson, time to react.

PHILBIN: When I watched the films of the Colts-Vikings game, I saw [Minnesota defensive end] Carl Eller manhandle Sam Ball, who I'd be going against in the Super Bowl. [Minnesota got to Morrall four times in the first half of the NFL Western Conference title game.] The Colts' whole offensive line had to call for help and bring in Jerry Hill to help block. I knew Ball had to be good to be playing in the NFL, but was he great? I had to draw my own conclusions.

BAIRD: After watching the films, I really wasn't so scared of the Colts offense. I didn't see anything to make me think their quarterback and receivers were as good as some we played against in the AFL, particularly considering what we faced every day in practice. When you practice against a Joe Namath throwing the ball to a Sauer, Maynard and Lammons, you're not gonna come up against better than that in a game. People didn't think about that when they made up things like point-spreads and matchups. They let their emotions run wild; let themselves be influenced by the past two games. The Colts beat Cleveland 34-0, so everybody said they had to be unbeatable. But I remember Walt Michaels saying "Look, I know Earl Morrall and you can't convince me that all of a sudden Earl Morrall is in the same class as a Joe Namath or a Daryle Lamonica or a John Hadl." So it wasn't only Joe thinking and saying that stuff. Sure, their receivers were good, but they weren't Lance Alworth. When I was at

Baltimore, I'd practiced against Jerry Hill and Tom Matte. I mean Jerry Hill wasn't as strong or as fast as Matt Snell, and Emerson Boozer was faster than both those guys.

MAYNARD: Billy's got something there about the practices, heh, heh, because Namath, Sauer, Lammons and myself all went to the All-Star Game that year. Covering us had to make our secondary better. But it worked the other way, too. Going up against guys like Sample and Hudson was no picnic. Sample helped make me a better receiver, or better than I would have been if I hadn't run against him for two or three years. Anytime Joe would throw the ball, I knew that I would have to come back for the ball or go get it just a little bit quicker than against somebody without Johnny's experience or ability. I'm just thankful he wasn't as intimidating against his teammates in practice as he was in a game.

The Herman-Bubba and Hudson-Mackey Matchups

HERMAN: I had been playing right guard almost all season and Sam Walton was playing right tackle. But Sam was a rookie and he wasn't used to the long season. It started wearing on him and he started making mistakes and not performing the way he did at the start of season. So a couple of weeks before the championship game, the coaches decided to go with our five best lineman. That meant putting Bob Talamini, a great run blocker, at left guard, moving Randy Rasmussen from left to right guard and moving me from right guard to right tackle. Now while I wasn't physically as big as Sam Walton [Herman was 6'1", 255 to Walton's 6'5", 270], the coaches felt that I would be more consistent. I had had zero experience at tackle; never played a game there in my five years in the league.

So I had to play against Ike Lassiter in the championship game and then Bubba Smith in the Super Bowl. Basically, they wouldn't line up way outside like a Deacon Jones [of the Los Angeles Rams] would, they'd line up a little bit on the outside shoulder. So what I had to do was take the angle away from them and stop them at the line of scrimmage, it was simple as that.

The thing that really made that even more difficult—and, yeah, it's a different technique, but if you can play the game, you can play the game—was the fact that they were so damn big. Both of them were almost 300 pounds; Bubba was 6'7". And you know how much anxiety that created for me? A ton, a ton, a ton. The writers started writing about it like they were apologizing to the fans for what was going to happen. This was supposed to be the mismatch of the year. The coaches kept saying "We know you can do it, we know you can do it." But I read between the lines. They were really thinking, "We hope you can do it." I really felt the weight of the whole ballgame was on my shoulders because if I couldn't block Bubba then we'd have to compensate for it. And if we compensated for it that would mean keeping Snell or in keeping the tight end in. Someone was gonna have to come out of the passing pattern and that affects your whole passing game.

Having a good game against Lassiter in the title game didn't do much for my confidence. If I had a bad game, it probably would have been terrible. But the Super Bowl was the Super Bowl and Bubba Smith had made a big name for himself. You know, we were both at Michigan State. I was a senior there when Bubba was a freshman and I didn't really get to know him then at all.

I just went through practice and always kept in mind that the way I was going to win the battle was by being fundamentally sound, doing everything the way the text book said to do it. You can't change your style because somebody's bigger than you are, even less so when they're bigger than you are because if you make a mistake and get off balance, they can just throw you completely off the line and overpower you. But I tried to turn the height disadvantage into an advantage. Our offensive line coach Joe Spencer decided that the strategy should be that I was gonna get into him right away. Whether it was a passing play or a running play, I would block him the same way: fire out into him and get my head right in his chest before he could get his momentum going. That way, I could buy some time for Namath. One problem for me was that I had a bad ankle, but I had a way of blocking any kind of pain out my mind.

BUBBA SMITH: I twisted my left ankle in the Cleveland game and getting ready for the Super Bowl, I didn't have the mobility I had all year. I missed time in practice, I wasn't able to really get my head into the things they [the Jets] liked to do. I knew that Joe had a quick release and I worried that if they threw to my side, I wouldn't be able to come off the ball, accept the lick and still be able to get into the air to block the pass.

RASMUSSEN: When they decided to move Dave from right guard to tackle, I was switched from left to right guard. Now, I'm not saying that my adjustment was bigger than Dave's—he was up against a tough physical mismatch there—but sliding from guard to tackle isn't as big a slide as switching from the left to the right side of the line. It's like batting lefthanded all your life and then you've got to start batting righthanded. At first, my stance wasn't right and it took a little getting used to. But by the time we played the Super Bowl, I was pretty much used to it. Billy Ray Smith may have been getting old, but he was a damn good defensive tackle.

I feel we handled their pass rush well because the AFL was a passing league and we stressed pass blocking; worked on it all the time. Defenses in the NFL were going against guys that weren't quite as good as pass blockers. That's why the Colts looked so intimidating and could play a basic zone in the back-field. But when the quarterback is getting an extra half second to throw all the time, like we were giving Joe, you've got to do something like the bump-and-run. You can't let those receivers just blow right off the line and get downfield that quick.

GRANTHAM: John Mackey was really the only guy on their offense who scared us. I figured they would bring Mackey to my side and play power football because Mackey was certainly bigger than I was [6'2", 230 vs. 6'0", 210]. He was a great physical specimen and, in my opinion, probably the greatest tight end who ever played the game. Kellen Winslow [of the San Diego Chargers in the '80s] is the only one close. Mackey could run, catch a pass, and block. He was the guy they liked to go to over the middle. Jimmy Orr and Willie Richardson basically ran side-line-type patterns. I knew Jim Hudson would have to play him tight and that I would have to help out with double coverage on some plays. We couldn't let him break a long one.

HUDSON: All that stuff about us concentrating on Mackey is a little overdone. Sure, he was the best tight end I'd ever seen, but in our game plan, we treated him just like another good tight end. I didn't feel any extra pressure to stop him. They kept talking about Mackey's size, but we'd gone up against tight ends in the AFL who were that big—Fred Arbanas at Kansas City and Willie Frazier and Jacque MacKinnon at San Diego—and we handled ourselves pretty well.

We knew from the films that they liked to go to him on third down and that he liked to line up in the backfield sometimes. The idea was to anchor the safety in the middle of the field to see which way Mackey was gonna go before he committed himself. But all of us in the secondary knew that the only way you can play defense back there is to get a good rush from your front seven [lineman and linebackers]. If those guys didn't do their jobs, it didn't matter who was back there.

PHILBIN: When I watched the films, I noticed that the strength of their offense was to their right, which was my side. They had Mackey on that side, so on running plays, I knew I would have to get ready for a double-team by him and Sam Ball, the offensive tackle. They were both big guys and great at their positions so all I wanted to do was just hold my position long enough so Ralph Baker or Al Atkinson could come across and make the tackle. Overall, I'd say that after watching the films we weren't overly impressed with their offensive line. They were good, but not better than the good lines we faced in the AFL.

109

troops. On the second play of the second quarter, and the ball on the Jets' six-yard line, the Colts missed another scoring opportunity when a Morrall pass to Mitchell was tipped by linebacker Al Atkinson, hit the tight end in the shoulder pads and caromed into the welcoming arms of Jets cornerback Randy Beverly in the end zone.

New York was determined to establish the running game on its next series. Matt Snell and Emerson Boozer ran four straight times behind Winston Hill for 26 yards and two first downs, putting the ball on the Colts' nine-yard line. Two Snell blasts later, the Jets were leading, 7-0, and 75,377 fans in the Orange Bowl were unified in their disbelief.

The highlights of the next two drives were Morrall's 20-yard pass play to Tom Matte, and Namath teaming with Sauer for 35, but both Michaels and Jim Turner missed field goal attempts from beyond 40 yards. On the Colts' next possession, they maneuvered into their third scoring chance of the half. From the Baltimore 26, Matte broke free down the right sideline for a 58-yard gain. Two plays later, however, Morrall underthrew Richardson over the middle and cornerback Johnny Sample intercepted the ball on the Jets' two-yard line.

But that wouldn't be the Colts' last frustrating episode of the first 30 minutes. After forcing the Jets to punt from their own seven, the Colts were again in New York territory with less than a minute in the half. On second down from the Jets' 41, Morrall handed off to Matte, who swept right only to stop and pass the ball back to his quarterback. It was the old "flea-flicker" play. With split end Orr all alone down field, frantically waving his arms near the end zone, Morrall threw down the middle to Jerry Hill. Jets strong safety Jim Hudson, who had picked up the closest blue uniform in sight as the play developed, lunged in front of Hill and corralled his team's third interception. The half ended with the Jets leading, 7-0, and the Colts having "blown" a chance for a minimum of 16 and a maximum of 24 points.

It was imperative for Baltimore to establish some momentum in the third quarter, but even that hope disappeared when Matte fumbled on the first play of the half. Starting what would be a

Super Bowl III. The Jets crossed up the Colts by establishing a running game. Here Joe Namath hands off to halfback Emerson Boozer. (UPI/ Bettmann Newsphotos)

The Baltimore Colts gang-tackle Jet end Pete Lammons after a two-yard gain. (AP Wirephoto)

four-minute drive on the Colts' 33, Namath went to Snell and Boozer on four straight plays before Bubba Smith nailed the Jets quarterback on the 25 for the defensive end's only sack of the day. It still left Jim Turner close enough to kick the Jets into a 10-0 lead.

The Colts went three plays and punt on their next possession, which would be Earl Morrall's last of the game. After a four-minute, 10-play, 45-yard Jets drive led to another Turner field goal, Johnny Unitas took control of the Baltimore offense. The great veteran had no better luck moving the ball on the Jets' determined defense than Morrall: the Colts punted after three plays. All the NFL champions had to show for the third quarter was 10 yards of total offense on seven plays.

Namath, who had missed the last play of the previous drive with a thumb injury, took over again with a little over two minutes left in third quarter. He overthrew Sauer on second down, then connected with the split end for consecutive completions of 11 and 39 yards. Though the Colts' defense prevented the Jets runners from scoring inside the 10-yard line, Jim Turner's third goal put his team comfortably ahead, 16-0, with just over 13 minutes left in the game.

The next time Unitas took the field, he displayed some of his old magic. Three first downs put the ball on the Jets' 25, before Baltimore again self-destructed. Unitas tried to connect with Orr cutting over the middle near the end zone. But while the master's mind was willing, the ailing and aging arm wouldn't respond. A throw which had to be fired down the field merely floated and hung in the air long enough for Randy Beverly to pick off his second pass of the day.

Namath played ball-control on the next Jets series and ran five and a half minutes off the clock before Jim Turner missed a 42-yard field goal attempt. With the New York secondary now playing for the long pass, Unitas completed passes of 17, 11, 21 and 11 yards, bringing the ball to the Jets' two. The Colts then needed four plays to score their first touchdown. Jerry Hill's one-yard run made it 16-7.

Those extra minutes Baltimore used to score must have seemed like hours to Colts coach Don Shula and would prove costly when they recovered an on-side kick at the New York 44 with three minutes left. "That's $5,000 a minute," said Jets linebacker Larry Grantham in the huddle, referring to the cash each player would get for a victory. After completing three straight passes, Unitas missed on the next three and the Jets assumed control on their own 20 with 2:21 left in the game.

About two minutes and 20 seconds later, Unitas threw a 15-yard pass which Willie Richardson leapt to catch at midfield. By the time he landed, the New York Jets were world champions, had pulled off one of the greatest upsets in sports history and insured that pro football would never be the same again.

Pre-Kickoff

HUDSON: I got a little angry as soon as I got to the locker room and saw the Super Bowl program. In some of them they had the Raiders statistics instead of ours. I said, "Damn, we get to the Super Bowl and the program's got the goddamn Raiders in it."

GRANTHAM: That program wasn't the only thing that got me mad. The day before the game there was an announcement that the AFL playoff system was gonna be changed. They were gonna have the first-place team in each division play the second-place team in the other division and the winners would play for the championship. I read the newspaper article to the guys. It said the owners were doing it so the best team would play in the Super Bowl. Hell, they were saying they didn't think we were the best team.

LAMMONS: Whenever we had an important game, Curley Johnson would always say, "Chicken ain't nothin' but a bird, chicken ain't nothin' but a bird." Well, of course, he was saying it constantly on our flight to Florida and before the game he was walkin' around the locker room sayin' it to everybody. "Chicken ain't nothin' but a bird."

JOHNSON: It was a family saying. I had an uncle in Dallas who was a car salesman, and if he didn't sell a car, he'd say that. So I just adapted it. "Chicken ain't nothin' but a bird, and this ain't nothin' but another football game and the Colts weren't nothin' but another football team."

EWBANK: I didn't make a big speech before the game. One thing I knew would get the players fired up was mentioning the Fred Biletnikoff quote that had appeared in the paper. He'd said the wrong AFL team was in the Super Bowl. So I said, "Next time anybody sees Fred, ask him if he meant Kansas City."

I also pointed out that some of our guys had been with the Colts, but now they had a chance to prove that they had been capable of playing for them. And I told the team that in the first two games with the NFL, the AFL lost its poise. There was always one big play—a turnover or something—that changed the complexion of the game. I'd felt Kansas City should have won the first Super Bowl, but they made a couple of key second half errors and lost their poise. I told our guys we had to avoid that; that the pressure was on the Colts, and that no matter what happened, we had to keep our poise and we must execute. Those ended up being the words engraved on our Super Bowl rings—"Poise and Execution."

DR. NICHOLAS: Before the game there was a knock on the club-house door and it was [Colts owner] Caroll Rosenbloom inviting Weeb and his wife Lucy to a party at his house after the game. Weeb was very cool about it. He said, "I appreciate it, Caroll, but we won't be able to make it." Then he came back and told the team. Needless to say, it got the players a bit more intense.

TURNER: Anytime a coach has a ploy to get his team psyched up he should use it, but see, Weeb didn't have to come up with too much. I mean, we read where Tom Matte had said, "I've already spent my winner's share on an addition to a house." We didn't need Weeb to say much after we'd heard that.

LAMMONS: You could tell Weeb was a little nervous before the game. He got up to tell us which unit we would introduce and got it all mixed up. He said, "If we win the toss, we'll receive and we'll introduce the defense. If we lose the toss and kickoff, we'll introduce the offense. Ah, wait a minute, that's . . . ." Joe realized he had everything the opposite way so he suggested we do it like in college. He said, "Ah hell, Weeb, just introduce the seniors."

SCHMITT: I remember talking a lot before the game about how much money was on the line. My regular contract that year was $17,500 and I had a chance to make another $23,500 just for winning those two championship games. You couldn't help thinking about the money when you're making so small a salary. But what motivated me even more was that we were playing for a cause bigger than ourselves, so to speak. We found that out during the week when so many players from other AFL teams would stop by our training camp and our hotel prior to game day just to say they were behind us. And I'm talking about guys we weren't friendly with like a lot of guys on the Raiders. Here was Ben Davidson, who was an absolute blood enemy, saying to us, "Go out and kill those guys. Get them for us, too." I mean if Davidson could get behind us, you realized you weren't just playing for yourself, your team or your family. You were playing for the entire AFL, to help the league survive.

DOCKERY: The feeling I had in the locker room was hard to de-scribe, even now, over 20 years later. Only a few weeks before, I'd been playing in Bridgeport, Connecticut, my career almost over, and now I suddenly found myself in one of the biggest events on the planet, with the entire country focused on it. My appreciation for what was happening was incredible, even though I felt stunned, in a daze. The thing seemed totally un-real. It was like being reborn, you know, like Phoenix from the ashes, all of those metaphors come into your mind. I was no-where and all of a sudden I was right in the middle of it all. It was wonderful.

117

I felt more like a fan than a player. I was in a mind zone. I was thinking, "Wow, there's Joe Namath. Oh, oh, there's Johnny Unitas. Can I have your autograph Mr. Unitas? Just wait a second, I'll come get it right after I come back from this kickoff."

BIGGS: I'll be honest about it. For me, going into the Super Bowl was a low for me as a player. I was really not up for that game. It didn't have the impact on me that it should have had. Not only was I playing without a contract, but what really pissed me off was the fact that I got no recognition for that sack I made in the championship game, which was no doubt the sack of the year. It was like hitting a grand slam home run in the ninth inning when you're down by three runs. Not that I needed anybody to pat me on the back, but it was hardly mentioned in any of the papers after the game. So I said to myself, "I can't believe I made such an important play to get us here and it didn't mean a thing." And I felt if a guy like Philbin or Elliott had made the sack, the press probably would have blown it out of proportion. But I did it and there wasn't even a note in a newspaper story.

ZIMMERMAN: I remember Johnny Sample in the dressing room before the game. He was psyching himself up with this strange ritual. His fists were clenched, his eyes were closed, and he was shaking his head.

SAMPLE: You better believe I was getting psyched up. We were getting ready to play for that day 20 years later, right about now, when you are sitting with your kids and your grandchildren and watching some football game on television. Then you can say you played in a Super Bowl, you played in a championship. I wanted to play on the first AFL team to beat the NFL. I wanted to get back at them, to even things up a little. It might have meant a little more to me than it meant to the kids on our team.

RASMUSSEN: When they introduced the offense, Johnny had Larry Grantham carry his helmet so he could run out without his helmet on. He wanted everybody to see Johnny Sample was in this game, especially the Colts. Johnny really felt strongly about that AFL-NFL rivalry stuff.

BAKER: Usually, when we went out for our warmup, I stayed close to Joe and when the crowd cheered it made it feel like they were cheering for me. But when we went out that day, I was too embarrassed to do it so I let Joe run onto the field by himself.

HERMAN: From the time we got to the stadium—people were standing around saying, "Ha, ha, here come the kids"—until we went out for warmups, you could see and feel the respect the crowd had for Baltimore and the disrespect they had for us. But as soon as we started the game you could feel the crowd turn.

AL DEROGATIS (Analyst for NBC-TV's coverage of Super Bowl III): Before the game began, Curt Gowdy and I were doing our usual analysis of the teams and I had no qualms about saying I thought the Jets could win the game. Despite the fact that they were such prohibitive underdogs, I knew from watching the Jets all season that they had a much better team than the Colts thought. I'd seen the Jets beat the Chiefs and Raiders and those were very tough teams. Physically, Kansas City was as big, if not bigger, than the Baltimore Colts. I'd gotten a chance to see the Colts during the season and despite their great statistics, I frankly wasn't impressed. For one thing, I didn't think they had a lot of speed. So the Jets were really going up against the aura of the old NFL.

I honestly felt that if the Jets could establish a modicum of a running attack, if they could get 10 first downs on the ground, they could pull off a major upset. In fact, I thought they were good enough to shut the Colts out. I had the feeling that Matt Snell would run well against them. I knew Joe Namath could throw as well as anybody I had ever seen. So if they could establish enough of a running attack to keep the pass rush honest, they would do well because if the Colts had one outstanding feature it was their defense.

I'm sure when a lot of people heard me, they were thinking, "Well, they're home-team announcers," because we broadcasted the AFL games. But that was a lot of crap, because I was as close to the NFL as I was to the AFL.

The Jets' First Drive: Snell Sends a Message

SNELL: During the practice week, we had worked on three or four plays we would start the game with, including the "19 straight". Weeb warned us against running sweeps because the Colts linebackers were so active. On the second play, Namath checks off [calls a play different from the one called in the huddle] at the line of scrimmage and changes the play to a sweep. I don't know if he blacked out or what. I looked at Boozer and we both realized Joe had made a mistake. But the man's calling the play so you gotta run it. We run the sweep to the left and it breaks clean for nine yards. That really surprised Weeb.

Anyway, that was the play where I flattened their safety Rick Volk when he made the tackle. I don't know if he ducked his head or my knee hit him in the head or what. All I know is they had to help him off the field. Volk was shaky the whole rest of the game. [Volk was eventually hospitalized after the game with a serious concussion that caused vomiting and convulsions.] I went back to the huddle and said, "These guys aren't so tough." That sort of relaxed everybody and helped set a tempo for the offense.

MAYNARD: Volk wasn't the only guy Matt flattened that day. Mike Curtis, who they called "The Animal," came on a blitz early in the first half. Snell picked him up and blocked him so hard he wasn't the same the rest of the game.

SNELL: Weeb kept saying all week, "I think we can pass on these guys, but we've got to get the running game going." We weren't going to come out and just throw, throw, throw, although we figured that's what the Colts would anticipate because they felt there was no way we could run on them. They had stopped everybody on the ground all year. So Em Boozer and I made a

Colt quarterback Earl Morrall throwing a pass. Number 86, Verlon Biggs, is attempting to sack Morrall. (Bettmann Newsphotos)

Six foot seven Bubba Smith vainly tries to block a Joe Namath pass. (AP Wirephoto)

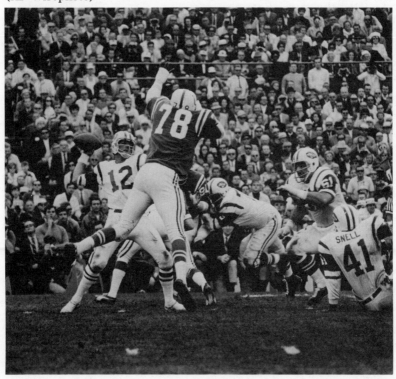

pact: whichever one of us was called on a play, the other one would do whatever necessary to make that play work. It just happened that my number was called a lot and it was working [30 attempts for 121 yards], but Boozer blocked like you wouldn't believe. He had some fantastic day blocking for me.

Our running game was geared to the left because Winston Hill was our best run blocker. We ran that "19 straight" play and had a lot of success with it all day with Winston handling Ordell Braase so well. The more Winston blocked on him, the more desperation you could see in Braase's face. Then the heat started to get to Braase and I think it wore him out, especially since he was playing with a bad back.

We had a variation of it called the "19 cutback." Winston would fire out on a guy one-on-one and I'd cut back off left tackle depending on which side the defender tried to take. It worked well for me because I ran better to my left even though I'm righthanded. I don't know why. But I don't think I made a bad cut off that play all game.

HILL: I didn't know before the game that we were gonna run over me as much as we did. But I was delighted Joe kept calling that "19 straight." There was a lot of responsibility there. And I had a lot of motivation for that game. The reason I was cut by the Colts in 1963 was because I didn't handle Ordell Braase in training camp. Five years later, I drove him out of the biggest game of my life.

The Colts' Blown Opportunities

GRANTHAM: The thing that sticks out in my mind the most—and I'd be the first to admit I didn't have a great game in the Super Bowl—is the first play of the Colts' first series when they threw a screen pass to John Mackey. Since he was the one guy on their offense we really feared, what we wanted to do was double cover him on every play and we set our defenses accordingly. Jim Hudson and I were supposed to cover him. But on the very first play, Mackey did what we call a "slow block." He hit a guy at the line of scrimmage as if he were blocking on a pass and then just drifted to his left. When he slow-blocked, I was supposed to take him by myself and just go up on him, grab him and hold him. But in the excitement of the first play, I drifted off of him about five or 10 yards and he caught a little screen pass and went about 19 yards. And I remember Jim Hudson running down the field and yelling some things at me that weren't very nice, things that couldn't be in print, you know. Because here I was calling defensive signals and I had blown the first coverage of the ball game.

PHILBIN: They were really moving the ball on us. They made three first downs in their first five plays. I started yelling in the huddle, "Hit somebody, dammit. We're getting embarrassed out there." Then I tackled Jerry Hill behind the line on a first down at about our 30. Then they made another first down, got down to our 19 and that was it.

EARL MORRALL (COLTS QUARTERBACK): Willie Richardson dropped a first down pass when we got to the 19. Who knows how the game would have come out if Willie had caught that ball? He didn't make the play, but it was one of many we failed to make that day.

JIM TURNER: They had to go for a 27-yard field goal and Lou Michaels missed it. That had to hurt them a lot, especially in a championship game because in a game like that, you can't afford to lose any points at all. When Lou missed that field goal, I could hear our guys saying, "These Colts ain't that tough." The game just seemed to turn right there. With each succeeding play, you could see that they were losing confidence and we were gaining it. And after that, quite frankly, the game was boring because we dominated.

GRANTHAM: Lou missing that field goal pepped us up really big. You know, Walt Michaels had told us all week that he had seen Lou and talked him out of a field goal or two. And when I walked off the field after he missed the 27-yarder, I thought,

"Boy, Walt's pretty sharp, he knows. He really did talk Lou out of it." And now I feel we've got 'em because we're over the jitters, everything's going to be all right. And now we basically knew what their game plan was and what they were trying to attack and we were ready the rest of the ball game.

WALT MICHAELS: I didn't really talk Lou out of the field goal. What I did was joke to the team about finding some way for him to miss the first one. My mom and some other relatives were at the game, but they were sitting on our side of the field so we had all the psychology in our favor.

RASMUSSEN: That first Colts drive scared me a little bit. At that point I felt, "Maybe we misjudged these guys." Of course, that's kind of ironic because that's what everybody felt the Colts were supposed to do to us. But it might have been the best thing that happened because we knew we had a real fight on our hands.

WALT MICHAELS: The Colts had another great opportunity when George Sauer fumbled a pass at the end of the first quarter. Baltimore's got the ball on our six-yard line and Randy Beverly comes up with that big interception. But what a lot of people forget about that play is that Al Atkinson tipped the ball when Randy was probably beaten by Tom Mitchell. Al got just enough of a finger on it to change the ball's direction and Morrall's throw came in too high for Mitchell to get his hands on it. Al had jammed his left shoulder the play before, but tipped the ball with his right hand. The ball hit Mitchell's shoulder pads and Randy was able to turn the play in our favor. That really changed the momentum because Namath came out and started going at them.

BAIRD: In any game you've got to get your tempo. As a defensive player, what you don't want to see is your offense go out and get scrunched, one-two-three-punt. That's very demoralizing to the defense. When we went out and made a first down on the first two running plays with Matt, right away we thought, "Hey, we can move the ball on this invincible defense." Then the offense doesn't want to see the defense give up a lot of yards right away, which we did. But when they got close we made a couple of big defensive plays, held them and boom, they miss a field goal. So we've regrouped and it's still 0-0 and I think that set the tone for the whole game. Panic started to set in on their side early, probably because that big point-spread put so much pressure on them to win big.

The Offense Takes Charge

RASMUSSEN: One of Joe's trademarks was his ability to change plays at the line of scrimmage when he saw what the defense was doing. During the second drive of the first quarter, he started checking plays at the line and that's when I said to myself, "Hey, Joe's got this game under control. He knows what's going on and we're in pretty good shape."

EWBANK: We always gave Joe a little more leeway in changing his calls at the line. Maybe that's why he learned so quickly. The system was basically simple. He called a color, and if it was a "live" color, then the real play would follow. Sometimes we changed it during the game. If Joe suspected that the defense was picking up the live color, he simply called "Check with me," in the huddle, and then when he came up to the line he gave a color—dead or live, it didn't matter—and the real call followed. He could change that one, too. He could say, "Double-check with me," and then he'd call two plays at the line and the second one was the real one.

He was calling practically all "Check with me's" in the Super Bowl game, and a few "Double-check with me's."

SCHMITT: During the season, Joe would call only about 15 to 18 percent audibles at the line, but in the Super Bowl he called at least 40 percent audibles. We knew that the Colts would pull their shifts and stunts late, that they would move around once we called our play at the line. So we would get up to the line, Joe would call a fake play, they would shift, then Joe would call a play that would go opposite the direction of their defensive strength.

Say our live colors or "checkoffs" were red, white and blue. If Joe called one of the live colors, the next signals he gave would be the play we would run. That day, we snapped the ball on one after the live color, so Joe would go through a set of fake signals at the line. He'd say, "Green"—not a live color—"Green, P-36-T," which was a run off the right tackle. And he'd say, "Ready, Set." And then the Colts would shift. Then Joe would call, "Red, P-37-T," which was a run to the left side. But the Colts had already shifted to the right side 'cause they would go with the way we set our formation. It drove them crazy because they couldn't figure out how the hell we were doing it. They couldn't pick up the fact that Joe was changing so many plays because we had so many different colors. They might be able to figure that "Red" was a live color, but we had "White" and "Blue" also.

Of course, you can't do all that without a quarterback who could read those defenses and people didn't realize then just how smart Joe was. They thought he was just a good passer. But his ability to read defenses was something you couldn't train. Either you've got it or you don't and Joe had it.

LAMMONS: I've got to throw in this about the quarterback reading defenses and changing plays at the line of scrimmage. Joe reading well and the other receivers not reading well leads to nothing. Everybody has to read. Maynard could read the defense before he stepped off the line. So could me and George. Everybody had to read to know where to go on certain pass patterns. Hell, if Joe called a particular play, we had certain things we could do if it was man-to-man coverage and other things we could do if it was a zone coverage.

SCHMITT: In the book Dave Anderson wrote after the game (*Countdown to Super Bowl*), he quoted [former Colts halfback] Buddy Young as saying I played the best game he'd ever seen a center play. Well, that was certainly a compliment and a welcomed one because people don't understand all the center's re-

Jets gang-tackle Baltimore Colt running back Jerry Hill. (AP Wire-photo)

George Sauer catches a long pass from Namath in Super Bowl III. Weeb Ewbank (in cap) intently watches the play from the sidelines. (Bettmann Newsphotos)

sponsibilities. You know why centers stay around a long time? It takes a while to learn the mental aspects of the position.

I wasn't only responsible for snapping the ball and blocking the middle linebacker or the tackles, I also called the blocking assignments for the offensive line. During the Super Bowl, between the cadence Joe was setting on the signals, we called blocking assignments up front. When Joe changed a play at the line, I was calling signals for the new blocking assignments at the same time. How did we keep from getting confused? The line signals were very short, explicit one-word calls—"slide," "slip," "pick," etc.

Anyway, the Colts had a blitz that had been very successful against NFL teams. The offensive lines would always get screwed up and the Colts' blitzer would come through and kill the quarterback. Who blitzed depended on what stunt [defensive switches at the line of scrimmage] they were using. So what it took to block it was five offensive linemen switching five assignments. We'd pull the off-tackle, the guy we weren't running behind, and bring him back around to pick up the extra man on the side where the play was going. That was the key for us that day—working together and being able to do things that we had virtually never done before, ha, ha, ha. And it worked. We were as astounded as anybody.

The Maynard Injury and the Overthrow

MAYNARD: I'd sat out the last game of the regular season against Miami with that pulled left thigh muscle since we already had the division won. If I played I probably would have tore it and would have missed the title game with the Raiders completely. I didn't have any problems against Oakland, but a couple of days before the Super Bowl, I hurt it again at the end of the workout. The Colts really didn't know about it because it happened so soon before the game and we had closed practices.

As I warmed up and went through the pre-game practice, I never had a problem. I'd kept a heat pack on it all night and nothing bothered me until kickoff time. I don't think there was any plan to use me as a decoy. Things like that just kind of happen.

DR. NICHOLAS: Don definitely couldn't run well before the game. I'll tell you something about Don Maynard. If he got an ache, he wouldn't move. But he never got hurt, even way back with the Titans, because he was very protective of himself. When he got his pulled muscle, his hamstring popped and he couldn't stride out quickly. On Thursday or Friday before the game, it popped again and he had some swelling. We told Weeb that he'd better use Bake Turner in his place. But Weeb asked me if we could use Don as a decoy, could he run at least one series? I told him he probably could.

EWBANK: I got Don, Bake Turner and Dr. Nicholas into a room before the game and asked Don how his leg really felt, asked him to tell me the truth. He said it wasn't a hundred percent, but it was good enough to play. I told him I had complete faith in Bake and that I'd rather have a healthy receiver in the game. But old Don just insisted he could play. When Joe overthrew him early in the game, I thought, "Damn, if he's healthy that's a touchdown." But I decided to leave him in because even though he didn't catch a pass, he was just as effective as if he caught 10. The Colts rotated their zone defense towards Don, double covered him all day, and left Sauer to work on Lenny Lyles one-on-one, and I'd say George was pretty effective.

DR. NICHOLAS: Don may say he wasn't hurt that bad, but he was bad enough that he couldn't sprint and Namath knew it. So Maynard would just run his patterns at three-quarter speed which is what they do anyhow on a fly pattern. His pain was mild, but had he gone flat out he would have ruptured it. That probably accounted for that overthrow.

MAYNARD: That overthrow wasn't any big deal. But I'll tell you, it might have been one of the few that were incomplete after over eight years of working that play, even in practice. Joe threw the ball well and I went after it, but it was just out of my reach.

You know what? That one long incompletion was more effective than three short ones complete because on that play I beat both [Jerry] Logan and [Bob] Boyd and I beat 'em bad. I was five yards down the sideline ahead of everybody. We might have missed seven points, but hey, whatever words came out about my leg being hurt, the Colts had to say, "Well, shoot, he didn't hurt it. That was just talk."

NAMATH (in '69): To a lot of people it looked like just another incomplete pass, but it really was one of the turning points of the game. Don had gotten beyond their bombproof secondary. He put the fear of God into them. It was a real show of courage on Don's part, going all out like that. But because of that one play, they kept up their double coverage; stayed in that strong side zone. That opened things up for Sauer on the other side.

After the game, Don came up to me, shaking his head and said, "Durn, I'm sorry, Joe." I said, "What for?" He said, "Shucks, if my leg hadn't been hurt, I would have got to that." Hell, if I'd known that, I would have thrown the ball two inches shorter.

ZIMMERMAN: Namath didn't want the Colts to start ganging up on Sauer, which would force him to rely on Maynard as his primary receiver. So to get the Colts worried about Maynard—and stay in their strong-side rotation—Namath threw some first half bombs to him [two], which is what you're not supposed to do against a defense geared to stop exactly that. Maynard didn't catch any of them. But he showed his straight-ahead speed, narrowly missing one touchdown and scaring the daylights out of cornerback Bobby Boyd and safetyman Jerry Logan, who had rotated over to cut him off.

MAYNARD: Because of all our plays to the left and the ball starting out on the left hash mark—remember that was before the hash marks were brought in closer to the middle of the field— for most of the game I wound up on the wide side of the field and anytime I'm on the wide side, I'll take the defenders all the way to the sideline and make 'em play my game. So when I went out there the Colts would have to show the strong safety Logan cheating over and favoring that side 'cause you ain't gonna cover me one-on-one. We always keyed the strong safety anyway and when Joe saw Logan going way out there to double-cover me with Boyd, then Joe knew Sauer was gonna get single-coverage. Or if George is not gonna get completely single-coverage, at least Joe will know that he'll have more freedom to the outside.

BAIRD: Why would our receivers have a tougher time against a secondary that sits back in a zone waiting on them, as opposed to the rough bump-and-run defense teams like Oakland played and which Sauer hated to go up against? All we had to do was give Joe time to throw and that type of defense was perfect for him. The other key was getting a lead so he wouldn't have to drop back all day. We felt if we got our running game going, it would really take them out of synch defensively, and it did.

The Jets Score First

NAMATH (in '69): I didn't have any interceptions, but I could have had one on our touchdown drive. It was a square-out to Sauer that went for about 15 yards [14]. I thought Lenny Lyles had an interception for sure. If he catches that one, he probably goes all the way and changes the complexion of the game. Hell, I was lucky.

SNELL: I ran the ball about five times in 11 plays before we finally scored in the second quarter. The two things I remember most about the touchdown was that I pulled a muscle in my bad right knee and how long it took me to get in the end zone.

I remember thinking later that it was a good thing we had hot weather because I could have the trainer put a piece of tape around the outside of my pants leg to take some pressure off the knee. It wasn't a bad pull, more like a slight twinge in the muscle.

On the touchdown run, it seemed like I was going in slow motion. It was a play that started on the right side of the field and was going wide left. As I got the ball from Joe, I wondered where all the blocking was coming from. I was going to run behind Winston, but I also had to read Boozer's block and figure out what George Sauer's guy was doing. Having all that field to work with kept it going a while. I wondered if I was ever going to get there. I decided I better take this thing in because I know Mike Curtis is coming.

People always ask me if scoring the only Jets touchdown in that Super Bowl is a personal highlight in my career. Frankly, I never think about it in that way. I got a bigger kick out of beating the Raiders for the title that year.

SCHMITT: During that drive, there was one tackle where Billy Ray Smith was pounding me in the stomach and I told him, "You do that again and you won't get up." By about halfway through the second quarter, we could see they were really frustrated. We could hear them cussing in their defensive huddle. They were starting to fight amongst themselves about why guys weren't getting penetration on defense. "Well, how come you didn't get through?" "Well, I had a man on me." "Well, so did I." "Well, one of us was supposed to be free." Stuff like that. They were just pissed off at each other because they couldn't believe what was happening.

RASMUSSEN: I don't remember much about the game, you know, individual plays. Maybe I've been hit in the head too many times since then. But I do remember that first touchdown because of the crowd reaction. You see, one of my vivid memories was of coming out to warm up. And it seemed the entire stadium was filled with Baltimore Colts fans, NFL fans. It was like the Jets fans were afraid to say anything. They were just very subdued. And as the game went on, you could feel that changing. The Colts fans were getting quieter and ours were getting louder and I remember that when we scored that touchdown, the place just erupted.

The Rare Turner Miss

JIM TURNER: After Lou Michaels missed a 46-yarder, we drove down to their 34 and I missed a 41-yarder. It didn't bother me that much at the time; I mean, I never felt that would be the difference. With our team, you could miss a field goal one minute and one play later we'd intercept, drive down and I could kick one to win the game in the last seconds. Besides, Weeb never let a last kick, a last play, a last interception bother you because he knew it could turn around real quick and it always seemed to with Joe. I always had to be alert with Joe because he could get us in field-goal range instantly. He did it four or five times during the season.

The Matte Run and Johnny Sample's Revenge

HUDSON: The Colts moved the ball pretty well in the first half without scoring, but that bend-but-don't-break defense was basically the kind we played all year. Really the only big plays they had were due to breakdowns on our part. In fact, when Tom Matte made that 58-yard run with about four minutes left in the second quarter, I missed a tackle two to five yards past the line of scrimmage or that's all he gets. I just closed my eyes and missed the tackle.

BUBBA SMITH: We practiced that off-tackle run with Matte all week because we knew how small Gerry Philbin was and we had John Mackey over there, who was one of the best blocking tight ends who ever lived. And the first time that we run the play in the game, Matte goes 58 yards, but for some strange reason we never ran it again.

GRANTHAM: Even though Matte got that long run, it kind of proved what we'd all been saying about Matte not being a guy who could beat you. I mean, I ran with him all the way down the sideline and hit him right after Billy Baird did. You know, I was in my 10th year in pro football and I'd slowed down since the days I ran a 40 in 4.85, 4.9. People at home asked me, "Where did you get all that speed to chase Matte down like that?" Well, I said, "He had my paycheck in his pocket."

HUDSON: While Matte was down on the ground, John Elliott accidentally stepped on his back trying to jump over the pile. When Matte got up, Johnny Sample was standing in his face and probably thought Johnny stepped on him and they started scufflin'.

MAYNARD: You know what's funny about that play? Even though I wasn't on the field, I'll be involved in it forever because on the NFL Films highlights of the game, they caught me on the sideline screaming at Matte, "You dirty Colt, you dirty guy."

HUDSON: Everybody was a "dirty-something" to Maynard.

SAMPLE: What happened was I wouldn't let Matte up. I gave him a little elbow in his neck. So he jumps up and we grab each other. I said, "I could've been in the stands and caught you, anybody could've caught you." He was mad, foaming at the mouth. Then a couple of plays later, when I intercepted Morrall's pass to Richardson at the goal line, I ran towards him [Matte] to give him the ball, but he turned his back and ran off the field. I told him "You're a chicken and you'll always be a chicken." He was upset all day because of that.

Again, that was my way of playing. If I could get the opposition mad at me and lose concentration, then my game plan was working. Shula knew I would do it. He told all the receivers and running backs, "That guy's gonna talk to you all day. He may talk about your mother, girlfriend, anything to get you to think about something else." But it didn't do any good.

On my interception I was right there, but the ball was thrown so much behind the guy, I had to stop and almost fall down to intercept it. I knew Morrall couldn't throw the ball. I told all the guys in the defensive backfield he couldn't throw the real deep out pass or the real tough slant-in over the middle. So we played for short patterns most of the day.

The night before the game, I dreamt about intercepting the ball with a minute to go and the score tied and running all the way for a touchdown. I was only mad 'cause I couldn't get up and run with the ball. So I tapped Richardson on the helmet with the ball instead.

I won a dinner with that interception. Lenny Lyles and I had been teammates with the Colts in '58 and '59 and we were opposing defensive captains for the Super Bowl. When we went out for the coin toss, I told Lenny, "If I intercept a pass, you buy me dinner. If you intercept one, I'll buy you dinner." I haven't gotten my dinner yet.

Later in the game, there was a play where Richardson ran a little five-yard out pattern and I pushed him out of bounds by the Colts' bench. Well, as I was running by them, I got hit with about six helmets. Those guys just pounded me with swinging helmets. If I had been on the ground, I would have gotten killed. I ran to the referee, who was the late Tommy Bell, probably the best official ever in football, and said, "What are you doing Tommy? These guys are hitting me on my head. That's got to be a penalty." He said, "You've been hitting guys out here all day and now you're gonna complain about somebody hitting you?" Made me laugh so hard, I couldn't complain anymore, I couldn't say nothing.

The Flea-Flicker of Fate

EWBANK: That flea-flicker they used at the end of the first half was my play; a play I had when I coached Baltimore. And all week when we were preparing against it, we never did stop it.

HUDSON: We practiced against that play because we saw the film when the Colts used it against Atlanta earlier that season. Walt Michaels kept saying "Safetymen, be aware of Matte. He'll throw the halfback pass and he'll throw it back to Morrall." When Matte got the handoff and swept right, I went for the play as a run because, for the type of defense we were in, I would have had to leave the tight end and be the force on a sweep to the strong side. But as soon as I saw Matte stop, I knew what the play was and went back to cover Jerry Hill.

Of course [Jimmy] Orr was supposed to be Morrall's primary target, but when he gets the ball, the first guy he sees is gonna be one over the middle because he's turned towards the center of the field to receive the pass from Matte. I don't think Morrall ever saw me to begin with because I kind of decoyed him and wanted the ball thrown in there to Hill. I went down on one knee and kind of hid. So I was right there to cut in front of Hill and intercept.

SHULA: That play was designed for Orr. Morrall was supposed to look for him first.

JIMMY ORR: I waved my arm when I realized he didn't see me. It's still hard to believe that I was that wide open. I was where I was supposed to be. I thought it was a perfect play.

ELLIOTT: The defensive line never threw Morrall for a loss, but we pressured him a lot. If you go back and look at the films of that flea-flicker, I wasn't but a half-step from Morrall when he threw the ball. Maybe he heard the footsteps and didn't have time to see Orr.

MORRALL: Ever since the game, people have said to me, "I know you've been asked about this [the flea-flicker] a million times ...." And I say, "No, it's a million and one." As far as whether there was a reason I just never saw Jimmy, well, who knows reasons. When I caught the ball from Matte, I was facing in towards the middle of the field and I saw Jerry Hill breaking down there alone. We'd run the play in practice a few times and you don't get the same reactions in practice as you might get in a game. In our practices, we found that Jerry would also be open on that play because the defense is trying to scramble back to cover the deep guy. The fullback was always the alternate receiver on that play. Hudson was covering to the outside and he reacted immediately. He raced across and played the ball real well to make the interception. It was a good play by Hudson.

SHULA: You know, it was the last play before half time and the band was walking across the back of the end zone. I think Earl never saw Orr because he lost him in all the blue uniforms of the band.

MORRALL: Well, that's nice of Don to try and get me off the hook, but I wouldn't suggest anything like that. I just missed him. I just blew it.

MAYNARD: I'm sure Don is just backing up his player, but all I have to say to that excuse is B-U-L-L. Besides, they always talk about how all alone Orr was, but I'll tell you what, if Morrall had thrown the ball, Bill Baird would have gotten back there and intercepted. Bill would tell you that himself.

BAIRD: We played mostly man-to-man coverage the entire game, but on that particular play we set our defense by their formation. Randy Beverly was supposed to bump Orr, then release and I would take Orr deep. But one of our rules was that if both running backs started in the same direction, we would "roll the coverage." That meant Beverly would take Orr by himself, I would take the tight end or running back, whoever comes up the middle, Hudson takes a guy on his side and Sample plays the other receiver. That's how the defense was supposed to play when Matte started sweeping to his right. My man was now Jerry Hill. As I saw Matte stop to make the throw back to Morrall, I checked to see where Randy was and saw that he'd stayed in the original coverage, figuring I was gonna take Orr deep. When I saw Orr running free, I took off on a dead sprint for him.

Time and distance now became involved. When Morrall got the ball back, Orr was pretty much stationary. They'd started from our 41-yard line so he didn't have far to go. When I saw the ball released, I had a sinking feeling because I realized Morrall was throwing it to my man, Jerry Hill. What happened on our end was indicative of how well our secondary played together as a unit. I covered for Randy and Hudson covered for me and intercepted. My contention is that had Morrall thrown to Orr, I probably would have gotten there. But all people ever saw was that isolated camera shot with Orr waving his arms, supposedly all alone in the end zone. A wide-angle shot might have shown something else. Since then I've told people, "If I was close enough to break that pass up then that will vindicate Earl Morrall."

BUBBA SMITH: I can't believe what people say about that play. Jimmy Orr was all alone, nobody within 30 yards of him. He's the primary receiver and Morrall didn't even look at him. He threw the ball down the middle of the field where we had one guy and they had four guys. And all four of them were there because they were out of position, which is what the play is designed to do. I'm not saying that Earl is the culprit, but his eyes never went over to Orr.

LAMMONS: You know why they made such a big deal out of that flea-flicker? To take the heat off of Baltimore for getting their asses kicked.

Atkinson's Pain and Other Half-Time Stories

GRANTHAM: Al had come out two plays prior to the first half ending and they sent in Paul Crane, who was usually my re-placement. I looked up and stared at the sideline. I didn't un-derstand why I'd be taken out of the ball game. And Weeb said, "No, Al's hurt. You've got to play middle."

You know, we went into that game with really only one mid-dle linebacker. Al was the only guy. We had a guy named John Neidert, but John came in from Cincinnati because he could run down on special teams and never really had the capabilities of filling in at middle linebacker. He didn't know where to line up by that stage of the season.

So I knew the two plays before the half they'd probably throw the ball, being they were down seven to nothing. One went to Jerry Hill for a yard and the next one was that flea-flicker. When I went into the locker room at halftime, my greatest concern was finding Al Atkinson because I sure didn't want to play the second half at middle. You can't have people lined up out of position in football because the other team will take advantage of it right away. And I was the only guy who could line up as middle. But I found out Al had a shot of novocaine or something and he played the entire second half with a separated shoulder.

DR. NICHOLAS: Atkinson must have gotten one of those injuries when you fall on the elbow and the shoulder pops out. We examined him in the locker room and could feel the collarbone moving up and down. Normally, a player would be out for six weeks with that kind of injury and sometimes we'd have to operate on him. So I told Al what the problem was and he said, "Tape it up, patch it up." I said, "Al, you'll be in pain every time you hit somebody." He said, "So let's get rid of the pain." Injected him with xylecaine, which I wouldn't normally do, but it was the Super Bowl, an exceptional situation. The trainers taped his pads to his skin and put a shoulder guard on him. He played the entire second half with a separated shoulder, and after the game his arm was bloody, black and blue all the way down to the hand. It was a remarkable display of courage.

JOHNSON: We had a lot of guys who played hurt for that game, like me for example. I'd tore up my right knee playing tight end in our game that year against San Diego [fourth of the season]. So I punted all season with a busted knee cap. I'd get it shot up with Novocaine before the games. Of course, after the Novocaine wore off, you'd hurt like hell all week.

In practice, I'd punt about 30 times, but after the knee injury I could only do about 10. But there was no way I'd sit out the Super Bowl. I wasn't gonna miss the opportunity of a lifetime. In those days, if you were hurt, you just sucked it up and played. But I paid the price. To this day, my right knee is just terrible. They didn't tell you about the long-term effects of playing with those kinds of injuries. You were just a body to be put on the field.

BUBBA SMITH: I was standing on the sidelines during the second quarter saying to myself, "I can't believe this, I can't believe we're losing this game." I even went in at halftime and said to Shula, "Let me line up over the center so I can change the blocking scheme." And he said, "Just play your position." I said, "Hey, man, it's your team." We didn't do anything to counteract what they were doing and I have no idea what his rationale was. You know, my father was a coach and I'd been around football all my life. So I thought maybe we should make an adjustment or two at halftime, like maybe bump their receivers on the line or have the linebackers help out. But the coaches didn't even talk to the defense. I sat by my locker and I think I smoked three cigarettes out of anxiety because of what I'd been seeing. I didn't like it and I was a little nutso. But the attitude was to just leave it the way it was because we're the Baltimore Colts and we'll go out and they'll be frightened of the horseshoes on the side of our helmets. I felt, you know, they're paid professionals. Let's get into the game.

MORRALL: Bubba wasn't experienced enough to get the coaching staff to make changes because he suggested them. We'd been moving the football well, so what are you gonna change? We were only losing 7-0 at halftime. Is that a reason to alter everything? We'd been behind in games during the season and won them. So what do we do now? Throw caution to the wind and change people's positions just because we're down 7-0? That's ridiculous.

When we went in at halftime, it may have felt to a lot of the guys like we were losing worse than 7-0 because we had just blown that opportunity on the flea-flicker. So we were ending the half on a downer instead of going in with the momentum on our side. That one touchdown probably would have wiped out all the previous missed opportunities. It would have been a whole different game.

NAMATH: I don't think missing that flea-flicker had a major psychological effect on the Colts during halftime. I think our whole first half did. They had to be feeling frustrated, but knowing that team, I'm sure they felt like the second half was going to be theirs.

As far as them making adjustments, hey, the Colts were touted as the most dominant team ever to play and they got caught in that dilemma all successful teams face—whether to change what's been working for you. It sounds like a cliche, but a lot of coaches believe in "staying with what got you there." In fact, before the game, Weeb said basically the same thing to me. I had had a suggestion to start the game with our two-minute offense and call the plays at the line of scrimmage. Weeb and our offensive coordinator Clive Rush didn't think it was a bad idea, but once Weeb thought it over he said, "I tell you what, we've been successful and I don't want to change much. Let's do the things we do best." And that's what the Colts did even though they were playing a team they hadn't seen the likes of in the NFL.

ELLIOTT: At halftime, Walt and Buddy showed us where we were making our mistakes on defense, where we were breaking down at the point of attack. They had been moving the ball more based on our mistakes than on their good plays. What mistakes were we making? Missed tackles, not filling the gaps and not getting penetration. They ran a lot of sweeps with the guard pulling in front of Matte, and if you get penetration you knock the guard off and the lead block is gone. We agreed that we were lucky to be ahead, but that we could play better football.

JOHNSON: When we went in at halftime, we all felt we were right about what we saw in the Colts' films; that we were superior to the NFL. Everybody in the locker room was saying, "Damn, they're supposed to have a great team? They ain't shit."

EWBANK: All I did at half time was tell Joe, "Look, we don't want to sit on a lead. Not in a game like this. Let's assume we're seven points behind instead of seven points up. And stick with our game plan."

The Matte Fumble and the Jets' Third Quarter Luck

BAKER: I remember it was a run up the middle. Matte was hit just past the line of scrimmage by Grantham and a couple of our linemen and the ball squirted out and rolled right to me. I ended up at the bottom of a huge pile at around Baltimore's 30-yard line. It was kind of a big play because we kicked a field goal on our next possession. Although 10 points doesn't seem like a big lead early in the third quarter, in the Super Bowl it is because everyone seems to play so conservatively. They don't want to make the big mistake.

GRANTHAM: On Matte's fumble, we were in kind of an odd-man line defense. I was lying up inside behind our defensive end. And he came in there, made a cut back, and I got my hand right inside his belly, just kind of loosened up the ball enough for it to fall out when he got hit. I really shouldn't have been that off-balance and probably should have made the tackle at the line of scrimmage. But then he probably wouldn't have fumbled. I enjoy showing that play to my son and everybody now on video.

NAMATH: I really think that fumble was the turning point in the game because it solidified our defensive unit. We converted that mistake into a field goal, and being up 10-0 made us more confident than at any time in the game.

EWBANK: I agree with Joe on that. I was worried because the Colts had moved the ball so well in the first half. I said, "Oh, boy, we've got to get this defense together," and when they fumbled that first play of the second half, it inspired us. Now we really felt we could stop them.

TOM MATTE (COLTS FULLBACK): We were a great team because we didn't make mistakes. But that day, we threw interceptions, I fumbled. We had a chance to have 27 points in the first half. It was right there, 27 points, and we didn't get any.

SAM DELUCA: I was broadcasting the game for WABC radio in

New York and got to know Howard Cosell pretty well. Anyway, I remember him coming into the broadcast booth during stoppages of play and asking me, "What the hell is going on? Why are they winning?" Howard was looking for answers and I didn't have an answer at that time, other than the Jets were playing good solid football and the Colts were making mistakes and that's how most games are won and lost.

AL DEROGATIS: Cosell was probably upset because he'd been saying there was no way the Jets would beat the Colts. He'd picked the Colts as overwhelming favorites, which really didn't mean a helluva lot. I think Howard ended up leaving the game early because he was so distressed over it.

SNELL: It seems that day was destined for us. The ball always bounced right. One example was in the middle of the third quarter. Joe hit me with a little pass to the left and I ran it for 14 yards down to their 38. But when Curtis hit me, I fumbled the ball and it rolled right back to me. No one ever knew I fumbled. Had they recovered, it could have given them some momentum and changed the complexion of the game. But we ended up keeping the ball for over four minutes on that drive and it led to a field goal, putting us up 13-0.

SCHMITT: By midway through the third quarter, our offensive huddles were almost fun. We'd get into the huddle and Joe would say, "Well, how's everything goin' guys." Then Winston would say, "Okay, Joe. Hey, I can take my man inside." The linemen would tell each other what they were gonna do to their guys. We would talk like that in the huddle and then go to line of scrimmage and call the play. We couldn't get out of the huddle fast because then the Colts would know we were running a "Check With Me" offense. So we had to stay full time in the huddle and talk about something. Then Joe would go up and call the play from what he heard us talking about in the huddle. Normally, the huddles were very quiet—usually, just the quarterback and the center would talk. But everybody was feeling so confident about what they could do up front, we were all sticking our two cents in.

PHILBIN: The third quarter was when I really started noticing the Colts hanging their heads. Late in the quarter they were looking worn out. We were a younger team and the heat was getting to them as much as the frustration. I saw it more on their defense than their offense. We controlled the ball over ten minutes that quarter and their defense was whipped. Our offense had pounded them, just manhandled them.

BUBBA SMITH: When they were up 10-0, I was kinda down because we not only needed a touchdown, but a field goal to tie it. But when they went up 13-0, I was thinking we only needed two touchdowns and we'd be ahead. I know it sounds funny, but in a situation like that you start reaching for things to keep you motivated.

HERMAN: Our first drive in the third quarter was the one time Bubba got through me and sacked Joe. On the play before, he hit me with a legal head slap that just knocked the daylights out of me. Back in the huddle, Joe called a play and I didn't know what my assignment was. So I get back to the line of scrimmage and I'm trying to figure out which way to block. The next thing I know, Joe's getting the snap on a quick count and Bubba's gotten the jump on me.

SCHMITT: Dave did an unbelievable job on Bubba, but in the third quarter, he got knocked so silly by Bubba he didn't know where he was for a while. We had to walk him back to the huddle. I said, "C'mon, Dave, take a break. Go out for a couple of plays." And he said, "No, just get me back to the line and I'll be all right."

BUBBA SMITH: We realized pretty soon we weren't going to get to Joe before he could release the ball. When I did get to him in the third quarter, I could probably have hurt his knee. His leg was planted and I chose to hit him up near his shoulders. I hit the turf myself and pulled him on top of me. I only did that because it was Joe.

NAMATH: I'll tell you, Bubba Smith was one helluva football player. One time I had Bill Mathis open and I heard Dave Herman yell, "Watch out, Joe," and I knew Bubba'd gotten loose. So I just threw the ball away.

LAMMONS: Bubba's sack must have shaken Joe up a little because on the next play he threw one of his few bad passes all day. We had a third and long [third and 24 from the Colts' 25] and I ran an out-pattern on the right side. Joe threw it a bit behind me and Jerry Logan got his hands on it and dropped it. If he'd intercepted it, he would have been off to the races down the sideline.

NAMATH: I should have never released that ball. I really forced that one when I should have eaten it. At least I threw it far enough away from Logan that he had to lunge for the ball and that's probably why he couldn't hold it. If I'd thrown it right at Pete, Logan would have intercepted and might have run for a touchdown.

Namath's Thumb Injury

DR. NICHOLAS: Joe had had a bad right thumb from the Oakland game, and even though Sauer caught a lot of passes on the left side, Joe was having trouble throwing that way all game. Anyway, Joe threw a long pass to Maynard that Don caught just a couple of inches out of the end zone, and on the throw Joe's hand hit Fred Miller's helmet and he dislocated his thumb. He came off for one play [Babe Parilli replaced him before Jim Turner's field goal made it 13-0] and we popped it back into place. I said, "Joe, maybe we should inject some pain killer," and he said, "No, then I won't be able to feel the ball." The adrenaline was pumping so hard he played right through the pain.

145

LOU SAHADI (writer, from his 1969 book on the Jets, *The Long Pass*): Almost forgotten in the excitement of Turner's field goal was Namath. "Someone catch me," he yelled in my direction. "C'mon, Lou, catch me, I've got to work this thumb out." We moved behind the bench in full view of the stands. Namath was 20 yards away and he began to throw. He did not throw lobs, but fired with the same force he uses under game conditions. I clutched each toss as if it meant life or death, realizing the importance of his being able to warm up properly and knowing that a dropped throw would result in valuable lost time. Namath threw four passes. Four times I returned the ball to him. Harvey Nairn, a receiver on the Jets' taxi squad, was then sent over to relieve me. On the very first toss Namath threw, Nairn dropped the ball. My fame was established. The crowd booed. Namath fired one more, which Nairn caught, and then Joe was ready to go again, his thumb back to normal.

LAMMONS: We knew Joe was all right when he came back the last series of the quarter and hit George Sauer for 40 yards [actually 39] when he went deep after a fake slant-in. I remember George telling me that Lenny Lyles said he was supposed to get help from Rick Volk on that play, but Volk was still pretty shaky from that hit he'd taken from Matt in the first quarter.

The Unitas Factor

SHULA: After the first half, I decided to give Morrall one more series. We were only behind 7-0, but things looked bleaker than that because we were the big favorites. The fumble that put us behind 10-0 certainly wasn't Earl's fault. But when we didn't move the ball on the next series, I told Earl I wanted to put Johnny in to get something started. A spark, a lift, something.

EWBANK: When I saw Unitas warming up on the sidelines, I was scared all over again. I'd coached John. I'd seen him do so many great things before.

HERMAN: You had to be a little bit worried. That was a legend

Jim Turner kicks an important field goal. The Colts' kicker Jim Michaels missed a chip shot field goal earlier in the game. (Bettmann Newsphotos)

Johnny Unitas throws a desperate pass with only minutes left in the game. (Bettmann Newsphotos)

running onto the field. Sure, they talked about his bad arm. But who knew whether he had one more great comeback in him?

SAMPLE: I felt the game was a little out of reach, but that Unitas was sneaky. After he ran out on the field, I walked over behind their line of scrimmage and told John, "Man, you know you don't want to play today."

DOCKERY: At that point in the game, Joe was the young legend who was leading us to victory and now the old legend was going to steal the thunder and take the game away. All the dramatic impact that writers and sports historians would see in Unitas coming into the game, and possibly winning it, certainly wasn't lost on us. All I could think on the sidelines was, "Oh, God, let him be rusty, let his arms be sore, let him throw the ball into the dirt. C'mon, clock, get moving. Please, move faster."

BAIRD: When Unitas came into the game, it didn't take me long to see that he still had his leadership magic. I was nervous when he came in because I could picture the Johnny Unitas that I knew back in '63 when I was a rookie. But after I saw the ball sail on him, I realized he just wasn't the same quarterback.

BAKER: That's when I really felt we had the game won. Morrall had carried their team all year and Unitas had arm trouble. If he'd been healthy and strong, he would have started, right?

GRANTHAM: When they put John in the game, our biggest fear was, of course, his history. We knew that Unitas had come in and won for them in bleak situations before. Our main concern was that we didn't get beaten deep right away. We wanted to use the clock and not let them get any momentum. We didn't really know what kind of shape John's arm was in so we talked in the huddle about our cornerbacks not taking any chances, playing a step or two deeper than they had been playing all game, and to just contain the running game. As long as it took them a bunch of plays to score, we didn't really care if we lost the shutout. We just wanted to win the football game.

After his first couple of series, we realized that he wasn't anything to fear, so we just started backing off and gave him a few short passes. Then we'd come up when it got down to the goal line and try to clamp down on them.

DR. NICHOLAS: Everybody still respected and admired Unitas tremendously, especially Joe. When Johnny came in, Joe started pacing up and down the sideline and even though we were up 16-0, he kept saying, "When we get the ball, we gotta score. C'mon, we gotta score."

The Colts' Last Gasp

JIM TURNER: I didn't feel like we had the game won until I kicked my third field goal to make it 16-zip at the beginning of the fourth quarter. Then we knew that they had to score three times to win. I was extremely happy about that particular field goal for another reason. It was a real bitch to make. It was a nine-yarder and remember, the goal posts weren't at the back of the end zone in those days and the hash marks were wider. So the angle was a real bitch. You only get maybe 50 percent of the goal post from that angle. A soccer-style kicker couldn't have made that one.

NAMATH: With a 16-point lead we were able to play a defensive style and give up the short passes. Even though we knew Johnny wasn't himself physically, we didn't put anything past him on the football field. We weren't going to give up the big play quickly and we were going to make them work for everything. I remember looking up at the clock and seeing six minutes, 11 seconds left in the game. That's when I got nervous, even though they hadn't scored yet. I was saying to myself, "Oh, Lord, please let's get this over with. We were so close to achieving our goal and you start thinking about being a youngster on all your championship teams—Little League, high school, college—and that now you have a chance to win as a professional. God, all of a sudden it becomes so enormous. And all that didn't hit me until that 6:11 point when we were so close to it.

MAYNARD: After we made it 16-0, I yelled to the defensive team, "Hold 'em. Let's shut 'em out." I really wanted to shut out the NFL after all those years of hearing how superior they were, how they had the best players, that we weren't in the same league with them. I wanted to skunk them and put an end to all that hogwash.

It looked pretty good when Randy Beverly intercepted Unitas after they had gotten down to our 25. But John finally got them on the board their next series. Oh, well, no shutout. I wasn't all that upset.

ZIMMERMAN: Right after Beverly grabbed his second end-zone interception, something happened that the TV camera never picked up and it was the biggest kick of the afternoon. Everyone was looking at a yellow marker on the field that could have been an official's hanky but turned out to be a potato chip wrapper. And then all of a sudden you saw Matte and Sample—screaming at each other from a 10-yard distance.

And finally Matte went berserk and charged, and John stood there like a guy waiting for a streetcar, until the last minute, when he rolled under the 215-pound halfback with a perfect body block and Matte flipped completely around. It was like a circus act, and Sample stood there laughing while the Colts tried to calm their frenzied teammate.

GRANTHAM: When it was 16-7 with just a little over three minutes left, I thought everything was all right. Then they recovered that on-side kick—the ball bounced over George Sauer's hands—and my heart jumped. You know, I would've hated for somebody to try to take my heart throb at that time, because it would have blown any meter if anybody ever tried to measure it. 'Cause then you start visualizing 17-16. See, as long as you're two scores up, you feel like you've got command of the game. But when they got the on-side kick down there about our 40-yard-line, we started thinking 17-16. And without having enough time for Joe really to get back into our offense.

So when I deflected the fourth down pass to Orr and we got the ball back with a little over two minutes to go, then we finally felt like we had the game. After I tipped the ball, I threw my helmet up in the air, but before it came down, I felt like a fool. There were still two minutes left, so I got humble real quick. But I knew that, at worst, it could only get to 16-14 and we'd win the football game.

The Celebration

HERMAN: When the gun went off, I went over to Joe and said, "You told the truth, Joe. Nothin' but the truth."

DAVE ANDERSON (from *Countdown to Super Bowl*): Thrusting his right index finger toward the dark sky, signifying that the Jets were the number one team in pro football, the quarterback hurried toward the dressing room. Wagging his finger triumphantly, he disappeared underneath the stands. There, under glaring lights, a television camera was showing the astounded viewers the sweaty, grimy, but happy faces of the world champions.

BAKE TURNER: I remember going into the locker room and yelling, "Hey guys, I hear we've just been made 14-point underdogs for the College All-Star Game."

PHILBIN: We knew [NFL Commissioner] Pete Rozelle was gonna come into the locker room, so a bunch of us started yelling, "Hey, Pete, you better take the Colts' names off all those $15,000 checks." That was really a sticking point with me. I was saying that all night long because I felt sure those checks were made out before the game with Baltimore names on them.

SAMPLE: The first thing I did when I got to the locker room was pull a newspaper clipping out of my pocket that I'd kept for two years. It was a story with Vince Lombardi saying that Kansas City wasn't in the same class with the NFL. When we won, I felt I could finally put that clip in my scrapbook.

EWBANK: I was just happy nobody carried me into the locker room. Two of the guys carried me off after the championship game. One was 6' 5" and the other was 6 feet and they ended up hurting my hip. I had to use a cane to get around the next two weeks.

NAMATH (from *I Can't Wait Until Tomorrow . . . .*): The only thing that really upset me all day was that after the game was over, we didn't have any champagne in our locker room. That was just plain ridiculous. Weeb and Milt Woodard, the AFL president, said that it wouldn't look right on television for us to be drinking, that it'd be bad for our image, bad for the sport, a bad influence on children. They were acting childish themselves. It was pure hypocrisy, and hypocrisy hurts our image a lot more than a couple of glasses of champagne. We were the champions, man, the best in the world, and we had Cokes and Gatorade to drink. The whole thing left a bad taste in my mouth. I washed it out later with Johnnie Walker Red.

LANCE ALWORTH (SAN DIEGO CHARGERS RECEIVER): I sat in the stands with a Baltimore fan on each side of me and they were giving me the business. Then in the third quarter the Jets started beating the Colts up physically and I kept yelling, "They're doing it, they're doing it." Lord, how I loved that moment.

LEN DAWSON (KANSAS CITY CHIEFS QUARTERBACK): You can't believe how great I felt when the Jets won.

HUDSON: When the game was over, we were spent. The pressure was all gone and everybody was tired. Nobody really celebrated after the game. When we went to the team party, there was really nothing going on, so some of us left and went to bed early because we were so exhausted. It was like, "Finally, we got this damn thing over with." I don't think anybody really understood the impact of what happened right away.

SNELL: Johnny Sample never had a drink in his life before the

Super Bowl. He had said that if we won the Super Bowl, he'd have a sip of champagne, so I held him to it. At the party we had in Fort Lauderdale after the game, he had one little sip.

EWBANK: That one game was a perfect testament to the nature of the sport. We were playing, I suppose, for an entire league. At least everyone else saw it that way. My players, my team, we did not have that large a focus. There was $15,000 a player at stake. There were the instincts of football in motion. And human nature—beat the man across from you. Especially if you keep getting told how much better he is than you. Sometimes you just respond.

SNELL: I'd never felt that strongly about having to win for AFL pride. But one thing really struck me after we won the game. Some of the guys from Oakland and Kansas City—guys who lost the first two Super Bowls—came to our hotel later that night saying, "I just want to shake your hand and thank you for proving we've finally come of age." To have those guys who were my peers come over and thank me for something I did, well, that's when I realized what the AFL pride was all about. That's when it started to strike me that we really did something pretty special.

NAMATH: Even though I hadn't been in the AFL from the beginning like Maynard and Grantham and Bill Mathis, I felt the sense of AFL pride. Absolutely. I felt a need to win for our people. Not just for the Jets, but for the entire league and that's what made our victory more special. We won it for the old Houston Oilers and the Kansas City Chiefs and all those AFL teams that had hung in there the first five years when things were bleak. Those were the players who had afforded me the opportunity to have a chance at a Super Bowl. And so when all those guys from other AFL teams were waiting to congratulate us, it made me feel as good about the game as anything. I mean, man, when I saw those guys on the Chiefs and Raiders feeling proud, I had tears in my eyes.

HERMAN: There were 11 of us playing in the AFL All-Star game up in Jacksonville a week after the Super Bowl and that's when we found out what we had done. I had some good football player friends like Ed Budde and Jim Tyrer from Kansas City, people like that. They would come up to you personally and thank you. It was almost to the point of embarrassment. "You don't know what you done for us, for our league, for our organization, for the game we're about to play." They were a good bunch of people who were struggling for an identity and we gave it to them in one damn 60-minute period. That was the prime example of a moment when the whole thing really did sink in.

ELLIOTT: I remember there was one guy from Boston [now New England Patriots] at the All-Star Game. I forget his name, but he said, "Man, I couldn't sleep at all the night before the game, because I was so nervous for y'all. You don't know how happy it made me." The Oakland guys, of course, said that they should have been there instead of us.

ZIMMERMAN: Clive Rush once told me that he'd seen Howard Cosell at the airport after the game and Cosell went up to him and said, "I'd like to shake your hand." Clive just shook his head "no" because Cosell had been trying to get Weeb and the whole coaching staff fired for five years.

RASMUSSEN: I don't think I really realized what it all meant until the week after the Super Bowl when we were invited to City Hall and Mayor [John] Lindsay gave us the key to New York City. I mean there were thousands of people out there cheering us and that's when I understood the magnitude of what we had done.

BAKE TURNER: Since I didn't get a chance to play much in the game, winning it couldn't have meant as much to me as it did to the other guys. But I did still get something out of our victory. After the Super Bowl, Jim Turner, Maynard, Snell and myself did a commercial for Score Hair Cream. We were known as "The Four Jets for Score," and we did a parody of a Johnny Nash song called "Hold Me Tight." It went something like, "I used to play the grease bowl, but I was just a kid too young to see. Score's the only one for me. Mix it with a little water, and your hair'll hold like it oughta. Baby that's the Score, that's the Score, that's the Score." It went over so well, I cut a record called "Anybody Goin' to San Antoine" and it was the pick hit of the week in Nashville in '69.

MAYNARD: You know, everybody's got great talk afterwards. About a month after the Super Bowl, I was at a banquet with some Colts and one of their guys looked at me from the podium and said, "You tell Joe Willie White Shoes we're gonna get him next year." I was the last speaker and I got up and said, "I'll tell Namath what you said, but I don't understand why you didn't get him when you had the chance. You lost $15,000 for each one of your players by not getting him last month." Then I ran off the stage in the other direction, heh, heh, heh.

CHAPTER SIX

The Post-Game Show

The morning after the Jets' shocking, improbable, impossible victory, the entire pro football world—players, coaches, owners, sportswriters, fans—was still trying to figure out how it all happened. As a New York *Daily News* editorial the next day proclaimed: "As long as football is played, this game will be written about and talked about."

And so it has. The 20 years since Super Bowl III has been the ultimate post-game show. Football scholars are still dissecting and analyzing the event the way scientists try to unlock the secrets of the universe. It is as if continual examination of the game will provide the definitive explanation of how the Jets triumphed and what football's equivalent to "The Big Bang" meant to the future of the sport.

The two-decade-long discussion has featured debate about everything from Joe Namath's selection as the game's Most Valuable Player, to the effect the Jets victory had on the merger of the two leagues, to whether the game sparked a major change in the NFL's playing style. There is no debate about the fact that the game led to an increased interest in pro football in general, that it turned the Super Bowl into a major American "happening," and that it earned millions for both the sport and the three major television networks. The latter ramification has spawned the dark side of the post-Super Bowl III analysis—suspicions that the game might have been fixed.

In his 1983 book, *Kill, Bubba, Kill,* former Colts defensive end Bubba Smith claimed he was told of a Super Bowl III fix by

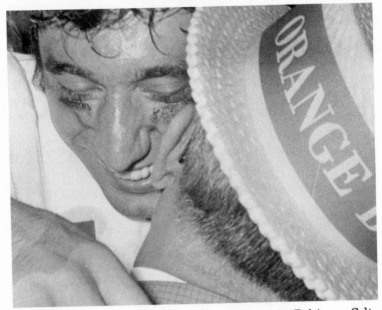

Joe Namath hugs his dad after the Jets defeated the Baltimore Colts 16-7 in Super Bowl III. (UPI Photo)

The locker room. Coach Weeb Ewbank is at left, Joe Namath's father at right. Namath had "guaranteed" a Jet victory. (Bettmann Newsphotos)

sources who went unnamed. Don Shula and some of Smith's former teammates vigorously denied the charge. But Smith wasn't the first to theorize that the game was rigged. In his 1971 book, *They Call It a Game*, former Cleveland Browns cornerback Bernie Parrish (who, like Smith, became an actor) took a cynical view of the game, pro football, and the connection between the two. After suggesting an elaborate scenario whereby the Colts' sideline could feed defensive signals to a Jets offensive coach, who would then relay them to Namath, Parrish wrote:

"Namath and his teammates' performance secured the two leagues, at the very least, $100 million in future television revenue. Considering other devices imposed by TV's need to lift fan interest and raise the advertiser's prices, perhaps it was too good to be true. What troubles me is that TV looks at football pragmatically, as an infinite number of unique program scripts. A Colts slaughter of the Jets would have confirmed the public's suspicions of a gross imbalance between the two leagues."

The implications being, of course, that a Jets loss might have allowed the NFL to back out of the 1966 merger agreement and that large TV contracts from the networks would have been impossible to secure. (Some have even suggested that if the Jets hadn't won, the country never would have gotten Howard Cosell and "Monday Night Football.")

It isn't surprising that few, if any, former Jets will dignify any claims that their victory was either fixed or a fluke. As many pointed out, their accomplishment and the entire AFL was legitimized even further the following season when the Kansas City Chiefs defeated the NFL's Minnesota Vikings in Super Bowl IV. The heroes of Super Bowl III don't appreciate people trying to devalue the ring they wear, a ring which symbolizes the ultimate accomplishment of a professional athlete. But there's not much they can do about it. As Gerry Philbin plainly put it: "It's great that 20 years later, the game is remembered and is still being analyzed. But that game has been dissected more than a frog in a biology class. It's really not that complicated. We were just the better team and we won the game. That's all."

Beverly is young and faceless. Edge Colts. Linebackers: Mike Curtis is considered one of the best players in the NFL. Dennis Gaubatz has a great-sounding middle-linebacker name, like Nitschke and Butkis. Don Shinnick has more interceptions than any linebacker in history. The Jets have some good boys, but Ralph Baker is slow, Larry Grantham is light and Al Atkinson can't be very good playing in the AFL. Edge Colts. Tackles: Billy Ray Smith is a punishing interior lineman who will intimidate the young Jets. John Elliott at 240 pounds is too small. Edge Colts. Ends: Gerry Philbin is a good tough kid, but he's kind of small. Verlon Biggs is an in-and-outer. Ordell Braase is quick and experienced, a symbol of the great Colt defense. Bubba Smith "is the greatest thing since peanut butter." There is nobody like him in the AFL. He will eat up the Jet line and use Joe Namath's legs for toothpicks. Edge Colts.

MAYNARD: You know what, I remember reading that Larry Merchant column when we got back to New York. Cracked me up, especially that part about Bubba Smith because I think one of the big keys to us winning was moving Dave Herman from guard to tackle to handle Bubba. Dave was outweighed by 30 pounds and he did a great job. Bubba only got to Joe once. So that's an adjustment that probably ranks as one of the high points of anybody's ability in any Super Bowl ever. It's just not that easy moving from guard to tackle because the blocking is done on a different angle. A guard is used to getting help from the center if the defensive tackle slides off to the inside. If you're at guard and he slides off to the inside or outside, well, heh, heh, he's still your man. You ain't got no help. You just hope Joe's done throwed it.

BIGGS: In my mind, Dave Herman was the unsung hero of that Super Bowl game. It's not so much that I appreciate what he did on Bubba Smith because I'm a defensive lineman. It's that the guy was playing out of position and had to make a difficult adjustment. Bubba was THE man for them on defense and Dave made him dance with him all day.

WALT MICHAELS: It wasn't like Dave Herman had a fantastic, unbelievable day and manhandled Bubba. He just kept Bubba from getting to the quarterback and Namath was quick enough to get the ball off. If you ask whether that was a good enough job, well, you're damn right it was because we got off the pass. Under the circumstances, Dave did a helluva job.

ELLIOTT: It seems like ever since that game, every year at Super Bowl time it comes out that Bubba Smith says the game was rigged. Didn't he say in his book a couple of years ago that it was fixed? You go back and look at it and see how many times he got to Namath, and if anybody rigged it, he did. I'm not saying he rigged it at all, but Dave Herman ate him up all day long.

NAMATH: I know what kind of competitor Bubba was and I actually took his claim of a fixed game in humorous vein. I really thought it was a joke. But I agree with John Elliott about Dave Herman. I don't know anybody on our team who played a better game or was more instrumental than Dave for doing such a great job on Bubba. And everybody knew Dave was having nightmares about it because he was switching positions.

HERMAN: Bubba could have adjusted to what I was doing so easily. What I would do was get into him before he could build up a head of steam. All he had to do was move back another foot and a half or move to the side a bit so I couldn't get into him right away, and it would have been a different ballgame. The guy fought a good fight, I mean, you can't blow him off the ball three or four yards. Why would you have to anyway when we had that mismatch on the other side with Winston Hill on Braase and we were running that way most of the time?

I ran into Bubba at a television convention in Houston in 1988. It was the first time I talked to him since the game. I said, "Bubba, I'm Dave Herman." He said, "I know who the hell you are." He was really very nice, but I'll bet you he's still not over that game.

BUBBA SMITH: You know, when I think about that game I get

to feel that heavy weight." That's just my particular funniness, you know.

PHILBIN: When we were at the All-Star Game after the Super Bowl, Pete Rozelle was staying at the same hotel as the players. I remember a bunch of us in the elevator with him. He congratulated a few of us and said, "You know, you're gonna spend the money and years from now you won't even remember what you spent it on. But the ring, that's what has the real value." And he was absolutely right. The money's gone, but nobody can ever take that ring and what it means away from me.

I used to wear the ring every day, I don't think I took it off for 10 years. Now I just wear it socially, for special occasions. Besides, I lost so much weight after I finished playing, I had to keep getting it adjusted. My fingers are shrinking.

SNELL: I used to wear my Super Bowl ring all the time and whenever anybody wanted to see it, I'd hold my hand out and let them look at it. Then one time a guy asked me to take it off because he wanted to hold it. Well, he dropped it and cracked one of the diamonds. After that, I put in a box at home where I keep it to remind me it's too precious to even handle.

NAMATH: Well, obviously, people know I was a member of that team so I don't wear my ring every day. But I love it, I respect it, I'm proud of it, and I wear it for special occasions.

Talking about the game isn't something I've had to do every day since we played the game, but it comes up almost every day. And it has always been fun and comfortable for me to talk about. I've never gotten tired of it. I suppose if I was a Baltimore Colt, I would get a little bit irritated hearing about it. But how could I get tired of talking about it? We were the winners. It brings back great memories and gives me a really warm feeling.

Although there are times like prior to the '89 Super Bowl that there were a flood of interview requests because it was the 20th anniversary of the game. I was just a hair frustrated until I realized that I should be happy that people are still interested in it.

My theory initially was, "Well, darn it, if they knew this was coming up, why didn't they call two weeks ago, three weeks ago. Why did they all wait 'til this week." But then I thought, hey, I hope they're still talking about it on our 25th anniversary.

JOHNSON: Anybody tells you they don't wear their Super Bowl ring all the time, they're lying. I've worn mine almost every day since 1969. That ring gets you in a lot of doors. It's helped me a lot. Say I'm trying to sell a guy something or make some kind of a deal with somebody I haven't met before. He looks down and sees my ring and gets curious. Then it's "Oh, you played in the Super Bowl?" And immediately he wants to talk about football and he's impressed. It makes things go down easier.

But as proud as I am of the ring, I'm bitter about one thing: the NFL not inviting us to the '89 Super Bowl to celebrate the 20th anniversary of our victory. As far as I'm concerned, Super Bowl III led to increased interest in pro football, helped the merger go through, and was probably one of the more exciting Super Bowl games. It was history and they should have recognized us at halftime or something.

SCHMITT: I wear my ring all the time except for when I go to bed. When I look at it, I think about being a kid from Brooklyn who was brought up in Central Islip, Long Island, and went to Hofstra University—not exactly a football factory—and who was lucky enough to be a part of the biggest game ever played. I just count myself very proud and happy to have participated in Super Bowl III, if for nothing else but experiences like our recent 20th reunion, which was one of the greatest days of my life. About 30 of us got together and not one of the guys had changed in terms of their personalities. Only a couple of them were heavier and most of them were lighter than when they retired. I laughed so hard just talking to all the guys again, it took my ribs three days to recover. It was just a phenomenal weekend.

HERMAN: My Super Bowl ring is far and away more important to me than that 15 grand that we got for winning the game. I wear it five days a week, put it away only on weekends. I was on

"In 1970, three years before I retired," Herman recalls, "cigarette commercials were banned from television and it created an advertising void for sports programming. The TV stations that Blair represented needed to replace the cigarette money with other advertising revenue so they set up a sports department. Kyle Rote [the former New York Giants star receiver and broadcaster] told me about the opportunity and I made a presentation. Blair was either going to get a media guy and teach him sports or a sports guy and teach him media. I'm sure that being a member of the Super Bowl Jets team helped me get the job. But once I had the position, I had to do something with it and I've been here for 19 years now."

Herman isn't the only former Jet who thinks being a Super Bowl winner opened post-career doors. JOHNNY SAMPLE, who was released by the Jets after the Super Bowl season and a year later wrote a controversial book called *Confessions of a Dirty Ballplayer* (which explored his theories of football and why he believed he was blackballed from the NFL), is now a tennis tournament promoter based in his hometown, Philadelphia. Since launching his "Johnny Sample Tennis Classic" in 1984, he has raised almost a half-million dollars and hopes to start tournaments in five additional cities by 1990. The 52-year-old Sample, who still owns a Philadelphia sporting goods store he opened during his playing days, insists that the tennis deals "could never have happened if it wasn't for my playing in Super Bowl III. When I go to talk to presidents and chief executive officers about being involved in the tournaments as sponsors, the first thing we talk about is that Super Bowl. That gets me in the door and the memories of that game seem to be getting stronger every year. Instead of winning 16-7, you'd think we'd won 200-0. There's no doubt in my mind that being part of that game has helped me since I retired. Look at Joe Namath's career. I'd bet that 80 percent of his income today comes from his being the winning quarterback in that Super Bowl. The game probably made him a millionaire."

"Well, I can't put a dollar value on it," says JOE NAMATH, "but there's no doubt about the fact that the opportunities I've had

John Dockery.

Dave Herman with photo from the glory days.

Walt Michaels at home with *Casablanca* poster.

1973. In the late '70s, Dockery entered broadcasting and was a sports reporter-host for New York's WNEW-TV (now a Fox affiliate). Besides working now as an analyst and sideline reporter for CBS television and radio, the 44-year-old Dockery is owner and president of Cambridge Office Services, which provides temporary help, trucking and courier services to businesses in New York City.

Dockery, a Bay Ridge, Brooklyn, native who now lives in the borough's Brooklyn Heights section, is also co-director with Joe Namath of an upstate New York football camp.

JOHN ELLIOTT was on his way to a Hall of Fame career after being named an All-Pro defensive tackle in 1970. But knee surgery in 1971 limited his effectiveness and he was released by the Jets after the 1973 season. He joined the World Football league in '74 and played in the new league until it folded in October of 1975. Elliott then returned to his native Texas where he served as sheriff of West Texas County for three years. The 44-year-old Elliott, who lives in Victoria, Texas, then got involved in the oil business and is now a partner in an oil well equipment company.

WEEB EWBANK coached the Jets until 1973 and five years later he was elected to the Pro Football Hall of Fame. At the end of the 1969 season, Ewbank was named head coach of the all-time AFL team. In 20 years as a head coach, Ewbank compiled a record of 134-130-7 and is the only coach in football history to have won a championship in both the NFL and the AFL. The 82-year-old Ewbank currently lives with his wife Lucy in Oxford, Ohio.

LARRY GRANTHAM was named an AFL All-Star linebacker for the sixth time in 1969 and retired in 1972 after a 13-year career. The 51-year-old Grantham works as a manufacturer's representative in Memphis, Tennessee.

WINSTON HILL was one of the NFL's premiere offensive tackles, making the Pro Bowl from 1969 to 1973. After being released by

Don Maynard's number 13 was retired by the Jets at Shea Stadium in 1987. (UPI/Bettmann Newsphotos)

Joe Namath at 46.

Gerry Philbin at his Long Island demolition yard.

(New York Post)

Randy Rasmussen at
a Connecticut
construction site.

Matt Snell posing by
his 1964 Rookie of
the Year plaque.

Jim Turner.

JOHN SCHMITT remained the Jets starting center until 1973. He played for the Green Bay Packers in 1974, before retiring and working full-time in the insurance business. At 45, Schmitt is now a partner in PFP Insurance Corporation of Milford, Connecticut, which generated $500 million in business in 1988. Schmitt lives in Brookville, Long Island.

MATT SNELL was named to the all-time AFL team in 1969 and retired in 1972. He currently ranks third on the Jets all-time rushing list with 4,285 yards. After quitting football, Snell had interests in a brokerage firm, a liquor store and a restaurant, and also worked for a company that represented athletes. In 1978, he started the Snellco Construction Company with money he received from selling his share in the brokerage firm. Snellco's primary work involves interior construction—either new or rehabilitation—and the Manhattan company had generated $7 million in revenue by 1989. The 48-year-old Snell currently lives in Bensonhurst, Brooklyn.

BAKE TURNER (the author's first Jets hero) was released by the Jets after the 1969 season and played one year for the Boston Patriots. Upon retiring, Turner tried to make it as a country-western singer, but dropped it when "I didn't become a star right away." In the '70s, he worked as a model and appeared in an award-winning commercial for Rango aftershave. During this period, he acquired his real estate license and worked as a broker before "the bottom dropped out of the Dallas market a few years ago." Now 48, Turner is a certified financial planner, advising companies on programs such as group health insurance. Bake says he is writing songs again and hopes to have a country-western hit before he's 50.

JIM TURNER played just two more seasons for the Jets after his record-setting 1968, but he kicked for another eight years for the Denver Broncos before retiring in 1979. Turner, one of football's last conventional, non-soccer-style kickers, shattered his big right toe in a game against Kansas City in 1974. Despite

1968 NFL Standings

Eastern Conference
Capitol Division

	W	L	T	PTS	OP
Dallas Cowboys	12	2	0	431	186
New York Giants	7	7	0	294	325
Washington Redskins	5	9	0	249	358
Philadelphia Eagles	2	12	0	202	351

Century Division

Cleveland Browns	10	4	0	419	280
St. Louis Cardinals	9	4	1	325	289
New Orleans Saints	4	9	1	246	327
Pittsburgh Steelers	2	11	1	244	397

Western Conference
Coastal Division

Baltimore Colts	13	1	0	402	144
Los Angeles Rams	10	3	1	312	200
San Francisco 49ers	7	6	1	303	310
Atlanta Falcons	2	12	0	170	389

Central Division

Minnesota Vikings	8	6	0	282	242
Chicago Bears	7	7	0	250	333
Green Bay Packers	6	7	1	281	227
Detroit Lions	4	8	2	207	241

Conference Championships: Cleveland 31, Dallas 20; Baltimore 24, Minnesota 14

NFL Championship: Baltimore 34, Cleveland 0

THE GAME THAT CHANGED PRO FOOTBALL

1968 New York Jets Roster

Head Coach: Weeb Ewbank
Assistant Coaches: Clive Rush, Walt Michaels, Buddy Ryan,
        Joe Spencer

NO.	NAME	POS.	AGE	HT.	WT.	COLLEGE	YRS.
62	Atkinson, Al	LB	25	6-2	230	Villanova	4
46	Baird, Bill	DB	29	5-10	180	San Fran. St.	4
51	Baker, Ralph	LB	26	6-3	235	Penn State	5
42	Beverly, Randy	DB	24	5-11	185	Colorado State	2
86	Biggs, Verlon	DE	25	6-4	260	Jackson State	4
32	Boozer, Emerson	RB	25	5-11	207	Maryland State	3
45	Christy, Earl	DB	25	5-11	195	Maryland State	3
56	Crane, Paul	LB-C	24	6-2	205	Alabama	3
47	D'Amato, Mike	DB	25	6-2	204	Hofstra	R
43	Dockery, John	DB	23	6-0	186	Harvard	T
80	Elliott, John	DT	23	6-4	240	Texas	2
48	Gordon, Cornell	DB	27	6-0	187	No. Carolina A&T	4
60	Grantham, Larry	LB	30	6-0	210	Mississippi	9
73	Hayes, Ray	DT	22	6-5	248	Toledo	R
70	Henke, Karl	DT	23	6-4	245	Tulsa	R
67	Herman, Dave	OG	27	6-1	255	Michigan State	5
75	Hill, Winston	OT	26	6-4	280	Texas Southern	6
22	Hudson, Jim	DB	25	6-2	210	Texas	4
35	Joe, Billy	FB	27	6-2	236	Villanova	6
33	Johnson, Curley	P-TE	33	6-0	215	Houston	11
87	Lammons, Pete	TE	24	6-3	228	Texas	3
31	Mathis, Bill	HB	29	6-1	220	Clemson	9
13	Maynard, Don	FL	31	6-1	179	Texas Western	11
50	McAdams, Carl	LB	24	6-3	240	Oklahoma	2
25	Nairn, Harvey	FL-DB	23	6-1	178	Southern Univ.	R
12	Namath, Joe	QB	25	6-2	195	Alabama	4
63	Neidert, John	LB	22	6-2	230	Lousiville	R
15	Parilli, Babe	QB	38	6-0	190	Kentucky	15
81	Philbin, Gerry	DE	27	6-2	245	Buffalo	5
23	Rademacher, Bill	DB	26	6-1	190	Northern Michigan	R
66	Rasmussen, Randy	OG	23	6-2	255	Kearney State	2
26	Richards, Jim	DB-FL	21	6-1	180	Virginia Tech	R
74	Richardson, Jeff	OG	23	6-3	250	Michigan State	2

72	Rochester, Paul	DT	30	6-2	255	Michigan State	9
24	Sample, John	DB	31	6-1	208	Maryland State	11
83	Sauer, George	SE	24	6-2	195	Texas	4
52	Schmitt, John	C	24	6-4	245	Hofstra	5
30	Smolinski, Mark	FB	29	6-1	215	Wyoming	8
41	Snell, Matt	FB	27	6-2	219	Ohio State	5
68	Stromberg, Mike	LB	23	6-2	235	Temple	T
61	Talamini, Bob	OG	29	6-1	255	Kentucky	9
85	Thompson, Steve	DE-DT	23	6-5	245	Washington	R
29	Turner, Bake	SE	28	6-1	179	Texas Tech	7
11	Turner, Jim	K-QB	27	6-2	205	Utah State	5
71	Walton, Sam	OT	25	6-6	270	East Texas St.	R
34	White, Lee	FB	22	6-4	240	Weber State	R

R—Rookie   T—1967 Taxi Squad

1968
New York Jets
Game Scores
(Home Teams in Caps)

	1st	2nd	3rd	4th	Final
Jets	103	113	64	139	419
Opponents	44	69	41	126	280

Jets	20	CHIEFS	19
Jets	47	PATRIOTS	31
Jets	35	BILLS	37
JETS	23	Chargers	20
JETS	13	Broncos	21
Jets	20	OILERS	14
JETS	48	Patriots	14
JETS	25	Bills	21
JETS	26	Oilers	7
Jets	32	RAIDERS	43
Jets	37	CHARGERS	15
JETS	35	Dolphins	17
JETS	27	Bengals	14
Jets	31	Dolphins	7

1968 NEW YORK JETS INDIVIDUAL STATISTICS

RUSHING

	Att.	Yards	Avg.	Long	TDs
Snell	179	747	4.2	60	6
Boozer	143	441	3.1	33	5
Mathis	74	208	2.8	16	5
Joe	42	186	4.4	32	3
Sauer	2	21	10.5	15	0
Smolinski	12	15	1.3	5	0
Namath	5	11	2.2	4	2
Parilli	7	− 2	− 0.3	10	1
Johnson	2	− 6	− 3.0	0	0
Rademacher	1	− 13	− 13.0	− 13	0
	467	1608	3.4	60	22

PASSING

	Att.	Comp.	Pct.	Yds Gained	Tkld/yds.	TDs	Long	Int.	Pct. Int.	Avg. Yds. Gained
Namath	380	187	49.2	3147	15/112	15	87	17	4.5	8.28
Parilli	55	29	52.7	401	3/23	5	40	2	3.6	7.29
Snell	1	1	100.0	26	—	0	26	0	0.0	26.00
	436	217	49.8	3574	18/135	20	87	19	4.4	8.20

PASS RECEIVING

	No.	Yards	Avg.	Long	TDs
Sauer	66	1141	17.3	43	3
Maynard	57	1297	22.8	87	10
Lammons	32	400	12.5	37	3
Snell	16	105	6.6	39	1
Boozer	12	101	8.4	23	0
B. Turner	10	241	24.1	71	2
Mathis	9	149	16.6	31	1
Smolinski	6	40	6.7	19	0
Johnson	5	78	15.6	18	0
Joe	2	11	5.5	11	0
Rademacher	2	11	5.5	6	0
	217	3574	16.5	87	20

1968 NEW YORK JETS INDIVIDUAL STATISTICS

PUNT RETRUNS

	No.	FC	Yards	Avg.	Long	TDs
Richards	4	7	57	14.3	37	0
Christy	13	1	116	8.9	39	0
Baird	18	6	111	6.2	20	0
Philbin	1	0	2	2.0	2	0
D'Amato	0	1	0	0.0	0	0
Hudson	0	1	0	0.0	0	0
	36	16	286	7.9	39	0

KICKOFF RETURNS

	No.	Yards	Avg.	Long	TDs
D'Amato	1	32	32.0	32	0
Christy	25	599	24.0	87	0
B. Turner	14	319	22.8	36	0
Smolinski	1	17	17.0	17	0
Snell	3	28	9.3	15	0
Neidert	1	0	0.0	0	0
Rademacher	11	0	0.0	0	0
	46	995	21.6	87	0

PUNTING

	No.	Yards	Avg.	Long
Johnson	68	2977	43.8	65

INTERCEPTIONS

	No.	Yards	Long	TDs
Sample	7	88	39	1
Hudson	5	96	45	0
Beverly	4	127	68	1
Baird	4	74	36	0
Baker	3	31	20	0
Atkinson	2	24	22	0
Gordon	2	0	0	0
Christy	1	16	16	0
	28	456	68	2

1968 NEW YORK JETS INDIVIDUAL STATISTICS

SCORING

	TDs	Rushing	Passing	XP	XPM	FG	FGA	Safety	Total Points
J. Turner	0	0	0	43	0	34	46	0	145
Maynard	10	0	10	0	0	0	0	0	60
Snell	7	6	1	0	0	0	0	0	42
Mathis	6	5	1	2*	0	0	0	0	38
Boozer	5	5	0	0	0	0	0	0	30
Joe	3	3	0	0	0	0	0	0	18
Lammons	3	0	3	0	0	0	0	0	18
Sauer	3	0	3	0	0	0	0	0	18
Namath	2	2	0	0	0	0	0	0	12
B. Turner	2	0	2	0	0	0	0	0	12
Beverly	1	0	0	0	0	0	0	0	6A
Parilli	1	1	0	0	1**	0	0	0	6
Sample	1	0	0	0	0	0	0	0	6A
Smolinski	1	0	0	0	0	0	0	0	6B
Crane	0	0	0	0	0	0	0	1	2
	45	22	20	45	1	34	46	1	419

*Ran for 2-pt. conversion.
**2-pt. conversion pass attempt failed.
A—Interception return.
B—Recovered blocked punt.

DEFENSE

	TACKLES	ASSISTS	TOTALS
1. Atkinson	76	68	144
2. Elliott	53	65	118
3. Baker.	53	56	109
4. Philbin.	57	49	106
5. Grantham	59	33	92
6. Hudson	51	34	85

QUARTERBACK SACKS
1. Philbin 19
2. Biggs 12
3. Elliott 10
4. Atkinson 5
5. Rochester 4
6. McAdams 4

1968 AFL CHAMPIONSHIP GAME
NEW YORK JETS VS. OAKLAND RAIDERS

	1st	2nd	3rd	4th	Total
N.Y. Jets	10	3	7	7	27
Oakland Raiders	0	10	3	10	23

SCORING SUMMARY

N.Y.—Maynard, 14 yard pass from Namath (J. Turner kick)
N.Y.—FG, J. Turner, 33 yards
Oakland—Biletnikoff, 29 yard pass from Lamonica (Blanda kick)
N.Y.—FG, J. Turner, 36 yards
Oakland—FG, Blanda, 26 yards
Oakland—FG, Blanda, 9 yards
N.Y.—Lammons, 20 yard pass from Namath (J. Turner kick)
Oakland—FG, Blanda, 20 yards
Oakland—Banaszak, 5 yard run (Blanda kick)
N.Y.—Maynard, 6 yard pass from Namath (J. Turner kick)

STATISTICS

	N.Y.	Oakland
First Downs	25	18
Rushing Yards	144	44
Passing Yards	256	393
Pass Attempts	49	47
Passes Completed	19	20
Intercepted By	0	1
Fumbles, Lost	1-0	2-2
Penalties	4-26	2-23

Rushing: N.Y.—Snell, 19-71-0; Boozer, 11-51-0;
Oakland—Dixon, 8-42-0.

Passing: N.Y.—Namath, 49-19-266, 1 int, 2 tds;
Oakland—Lamonica, 47-20-401, 0 int, 1 td.

Receiving: N.Y.—Sauer, 7-70-0 td; Maynard 6-118-2 tds;
Lammons, 4-52-1 td;
Oakland—Biletnikoff, 7-190-1 td; Dixon, 5-48-0 td;
Cannon, 4-69-0 td, Wells, 3-83-0 td.

Super Bowl III Statistics and Play-by-Play

Teams: New York Jets (Visitors) vs. Baltimore Colts (Home)
Date: Sunday, January 12, 1969; Time: 3:05 EDT; Network: NBC
Site: Orange Bowl, Miami, Florida; Weather: Partly Cloudy, 73 degrees, wind north at 12 mph
Officials: Tom Bell, referee; Walt Parker, umpire; Cal Lepore, line judge; George Murphy, linesman; Jack Reader, back judge; Joe Gonzales; field judge
Attendance: 75,377; Time of Game: 2:44

LINEUPS

Jets Offense		*Jets Defense*	
E	Sauer	LE	Philbin
LT	Hill	LT	Rochester
LG	Talamini	RT	Elliott
C	Schmitt	RE	Biggs
RG	Rasmussen	LLB	Baker
RT	Herman	MLB	Atkinson
TE	Lammons	RLB	Grantham
QB	Namath	LC	Sample
FL	Maynard	RC	Beverly
RB	Boozer	SS	Hudson
RB	Snell	FS	Baird

Substitutions: Mathis, B. Turner, Richardson, D'Amato, Johnson (P), Rademacher, Richards, Dockery, Walton, Smolinski, Crane, Neidert, Parilli, J. Turner (K), McAdams, Christy

Colts Offense		*Colts Defense*	
E	Orr	LE	Bubba Smith
LT	Vogel	LT	B.R. Smith
LG	Ressler	RT	Miller
C	Curry	RE	Braase
RG	Sullivan	LLB	Curtis
RT	Ball	MLB	Gaubatz
TE	Mackey	RLB	Shinnick
QB	Morrall	LC	Boyd
FL	Richardson	RC	Lyles
RB	Matte	SS	Logan
RB	Hill	FS	Volk

Substitutions: J. Williams, Mitchell, Austin, Hawkins, Perkins, Cole, Szymanski, Porter, Michaels (K), Hilton, Brown, Pearson, Stukes, Johnson, S. Williams, Lee (P), Unitas

	1st	*2nd*	*3rd*	*4th*	*Total*
New York Jets	0	7	6	3	16
Baltimore Colts	0	0	0	7	7

SCORING SUMMARY

Team	Period	Elapsed	Detail of scoring plays	Visitor	Home
N.Y.	2	5:57	Snell, 4-yard run, Turner kick	7	0
N.Y.	3	4:52	Turner, 32-yard field goal	10	0
N.Y.	3	11:02	Turner, 30-yard field goal	13	0
N.Y.	4	1:34	Turner, 9-yard field goal	16	0
Baltimore	4	11:41	Hill, 1-yard run, Michaels kick	16	7

FINAL SUPER BOWL III TEAM STATISTICS

	Jets	Colts
Total First Downs	21	18
First Downs Rushing	10	7
First Downs Passing	10	9
First Downs by Penalty	1	2
Total Offensive Yardage	337	324
Total Number Offense Plays	74	64
Average Gain Per Offensive Play	4.5	5.1
Net Rushing Yardage	142	143
Total Rushing Plays	43	23
Average Gain Per Rushing Play	3.3	6.2
Net Passing Yardage	195	181
Gross Yards Gained Passing	206	181
Times Thrown and Yards Lost	2-11	0-0
Passes Attempts, Completions, Interceptions	29-17-0	41-17-4
Average Gain Per Pass Play	6.4	4.4
Punts—Number and Average	4-38.8	3-44.3
Had Blocked	0	0
Fumbles—Number and Lost	1-1	1-1
Penalties—Number and Yards	5-28	3-23
Total Return Yardage	34	139
Number and Yards Punt Returns	1-0	4-34
Number and Yards Kickoff Returns	1-25	4-105
Number and Yards Intercept Returns	4-9	0-0
Number and Yards Misc. Returns	0	0

Rushing: N.Y.—Snell, 30-121-1 td; Boozer, 10-19-0; Mathis, 3-2-0; Baltimore—Matte, 11-116-0; Hill, 9-29-1 td, Morrall, 2-(-2)-0; Unitas, 1-0-0.

Passing: N.Y.—Namath, 28-17-206-0 int-0 td; Parilli, 1-0-0-0-0; Baltimore—Morrall, 17-6-71-3 int-0 td; Unitas, 24-11-110-1 int-0

Receiving: N.Y.—Sauer, 8-133-0; Snell, 4-40-0; Mathis, 3-20-0, Lammons, 2-13-0; Baltimore—Richardson, 6-58-0; Orr, 3-42-0; Mackey, 3-35-0; Matte, 2-30-0; Mitchell, 1-15-0

Interceptions: N.Y.—Beverly 2, Sample 1, Hudson 1; Baltimore—None

Punting: N.Y.—Johnson 4-38.8, long-39;
       Baltimore—Lee 3-44.3, long-51

Tackles and Assists: N.Y.—Hudson 3-3, Sample 5-0, Richards 2-0, Beverly 4-0, Baird 5-2, D'Amato 1-0, McAdams 2-0, Baker 3-1, Crane 1-0, Grantham 3-0, Atkinson 4-4, Neidert 1-0, Elliott 3-1, Philbin 2-0, Biggs 4-0, Snell 1-0;

       Baltimore—Logan 3-1, Volk 4-2, Curtis 5-0, Austin 1-0, Boyd 2-2, Lyles 11-2, Gaubatz 10-1, Porter 1-1, S. Williams 1-0, Shinnick 8-1, B.R. Smith 4-2, Miller 3-5, Bubba Smith 6-0, Michaels 0-2, Braase 0-2, Hawkins 1-1

SUPER BOWL III PLAY-BY-PLAY

FIRST QUARTER

Michaels kicks off two-yards deep in New York end zone. Christy returns to New York 23 (Hawkins tackle)

14:45

1/10	NY 23	Snell left for 3 (Shinnick)
2/7	NY 26	Snell left for 9 (Volk) 1st down
1/10	NY 35	Boozer right for loss of 4 (Shinnick)
2/14	NY 31	Namath to Snell for 9 (Boyd)
3/5	NY 40	Snell middle on draw for loss of 2 (Miller)
4/7	NY 38	Johnson punts to BA18 (Baltimore offsides, loss of 5)
4/2	NY 43	Johnson punts to BA18. Brown returns to BA 27 (McAdams)

10:55

1/10	BA 27	Morrall to Mackey for 19 (Elliot) 1st down
1/10	BA 46	Matte sweeps right for 10 (Baker) 1st down
1/10	NY 44	Hill sweeps left for 7 (Hudson)
2/3	NY 37	Matte left for 1 (Elliott)
3/2	NY 36	Hill right for 5 (Baird) 1st down
1/10	NY 31	Hill right for loss of 3 (Philbin)
2/13	NY 34	Morrall incomplete short to Orr
3/13	NY 34	Morrall to Mitchell for 15 (Baird) 1st down
1/10	NY 19	Morrall incomplete to Richardson—drop
2/10	NY 19	Morrall incomplete to Mitchell—overthrown
3/10	NY 19	Morrall back to pass, scrambles for no gain (Atkinson)
4/10	NY 19	Michaels misses 27-yard field goal attempt

5:33

1/10	NY 20	Namath incomplete to Snell—drop
2/10	NY 20	Namath to Lammons for 2 (Lyles)
3/8	NY 22	Namath to Mathis for 13 (Gaubatz) 1st down
1/10	NY 35	Namath incomplete to Maynard—deep, overthrown
2/10	NY 35	Namath to Sauer for 6 (Lyles)
3/4	NY 41	Namath incomplete to Sauer (overthrown)
4/4	NY 41	Johnson punts to BA 21. Brown returns to BA 42 (Snell)

3:05

1/10	BA 42	Morrall incomplete to Mackey—drop
2/10	BA 42	Hill up the middle for 3 (Elliott)
3/7	BA 45	Morrall incomplete to Richardson (broken up by Sample)
4/7	BA 45	Lee punts to NY 4 where ball rolls dead.

1:58

1/10	NY 4	Snell right for 4 (Shinnick)
2/6	NY 8	Snell right on draw for 5 (Gaubatz)
3/1	NY 13	Namath to Sauer, fumbles, recovered by Porter at NY 12

0:14

1/10	NY 12	Hill left for loss of 1 (Philbin)

END OF FIRST QUARTER: NEW YORK 0 BALTIMORE 0

SECOND QUARTER

15:00

2/11	NY 13	Matte sweeps left for 7 (Beverly)
3/4	NY 6	Morrall pass to Mitchell deflected by Atkinson, ball hits Mitchell in shoulder, intercepted in end zone by Beverly.

14:09

1/10	NY 20	Snell left for 1 (Braase)
2/9	NY 21	Snell left for 7 (Shinnick)
3/2	NY 28	Snell left for 6 (Lyles) 1st down
1/10	NY 34	Snell on draw, runs left end for 12 (Lyles) 1st down
1/10	NY 46	Namath incomplete to Sauer (broken up by Shinnick)
2/10	NY 46	Namath to Mathis for 6 (Bubba Smith)
3/4	BA 48	Namath to Sauer for 14 (Lyles) 1st down
1/10	BA 34	Namath to Sauer for 11 (Volk) 1st down
1/10	BA 23	Boozer right for 2 (Shinnick)

2/8	BA 21	Namath to Snell for 12 (Gaubatz) 1st down
1/10	BA 9	Snell right for 5 (B.R. Smith)
2/5	BA 4	Snell left for the touchdown
		J. Turner kicks PAT

Score: New York 7 Baltimore 0 Time of drive: 5:57
Johnson kicks off to BA2. Pearson returns to BA28 (Richards)
8:43

1/10	BA 28	Morrall incomplete to Richardson (overthrown)
2/10	BA 28	Morrall to Matte for 30 (Hudson) 1st down
1/10	NY 42	Hill right for 4 (Atkinson)
2/6	NY 38	Matte right for no gain (Biggs)
3/6	NY 38	Morrall incomplete to Mackey (broken up by Sample)
4/6	NY 38	Michaels misses 46-yard field goal attempt

6:37

1/10	NY 20	Boozer right for 1 (Logan)
2/9	NY 21	Namath to Sauer for 35 (Lyles) 1st down
1/10	BA 44	Snell left for 9 (Gaubatz)
2/1	BA 35	Snell dives middle for 3 (Shinnick)
1/10	BA 32	Namath incomplete to Maynard—overthrown
2/10	BA 32	Namath incomplete short to B. Turner
3/10	BA 32	Namath sacked for loss of 2 (Gaubatz)
4/12	BA 34	J. Turner missed 41-yard field goal attempt

4:13

1/10	BA 20	Morrall to Richardson for 6 (Sample)
2/4	BA 26	Matte runs right end for 58 (Baird) 1st down
1/10	NY 16	Hill left for 1 (Atkinson, Hudson)
2/9	NY 15	Morrall pass to Richardson intercepted by Sample at NY 2

2:00

1/10	NY 2	Snell left for 2 (Shinnick)
2/8	NY 4	Snell left for 3 (Miller)
3/5	NY 7	(1:12) Snell on draw left for no gain (Bubba Smith)
4/5	NY 7	(1:04) Johnson punts to NY 39 (Brown fair catch). Illegal procedure against NY offsets roughing kicker against Baltimore—no play.
4/5	NY 7	(0:57) Johnson punts to NY 46. Brown returns to NY 42 (Neidert)

0:43

| 1/10 | NY 42 | Morrall to Hill for 1 (Crane) |
| 2/9 | NY 41 | (0:25) Morrall hands off the Matte. Matte runs right |

206

stops, passes back to Morrall, whose pass to Hill is intercepted by Hudson at NY 12. Returns to NY 21 where he fell.

END OF FIRST HALF: NEW YORK 7 BALTIMORE 0

THIRD QUARTER

Johnson kicks off to BA goal line. Brown returns to BA 25 (Smolinski) *14:51*

1/10	BA 25	Matte runs off right tackle, stopped by Rochester, fumbles. Ball recovered by Baker at BA 33

14:25

1/10	BA 33	Boozer left for 8 (Volk)
2/2	BA 25	Snell right for 4 (Bubba Smith) 1st down
1/10	BA 21	Boozer left for 2 (Curtis)
2/8	BA 19	Namath to Snell for 5 (Curtis)
3/3	BA 14	Snell right for 3 (Gaubatz) 1st down
1/10	BA 11	Boozer left end for loss of 5 (Lyles)
2/15	BA 16	Namath sacked for loss of 9 (Bubba Smith)
3/24	BA 25	Namath incomplete to Lammons (broken up by Logan)
4/24	BA 25	J. Turner kicks 32-yard field goal

Score: New York 10 Baltimore 0

Johnson kicks off to BA 5. Brown returns to BA 26 (D'Amato) *9:58*

1/10	BA 26	Morrall incomplete to Mackey—overthrown
2/10	BA 26	Morrall to Hill for no gain (Grantham)
3/10	BA 26	Morrall sacked for loss of 2 (McAdams)
4/12	BA 24	Lee punts to NY 32. Baird no return (S. Williams)

8:04

1/10	NY 32	Namath to Mathis for 1 (Curtis)
2/9	NY 33	Namath to Sauer for 14 (Volk) 1st down
1/10	NY 47	Namath incomplete to Maynard—overthrown
2/10	NY 47	Boozer left for 4 (B.R. Smith)
3/7	BA 49	Namath to Lammons for 11 (Logan) 1st down
1/10	BA 38	Namath incomplete to Maynard—overthrown
2/10	BA 38	Namath to Snell for 14 (Curtis) 1st down
1/10	BA 24	Mathis up middle on draw for 1 (Shinnick)
2/9	BA 23	Namath incomplete to Maynard (caught out of end zone). Namath hurt on play, replaced by Parilli.
3/9	BA 23	Parilli incomplete short to Sauer

4/9   BA 23   J. Turner kicks 30-yard field goal.
Score: New York 13 Baltimore 0

Johnson kicks off—hits goalposts
3:51
1/10   BA 20   Matte sweeps right for 5 (Baker)
2/5   BA 25   Unitas to Matte for no gain (Grantham)
2/5   BA 25   Unitas incomplete to Orr—dropped
4/5   BA 25   Lee punts to NY 37. Baird fair catch
2:24
1/10   NY 37   Snell left for 3 (B.R. Smith)
2/7   NY 40   Namath incomplete to Sauer—overthrown
3/7   NY 40   Namath to Sauer for 11 (Lyles) 1st down
1/10   BA 49   Namath to Sauer for 39 (Lyles) 1st down
1/10   BA 10   Snell right for 4 (Gaubatz)
2/6   BA 6
END OF THE QUARTER

FOURTH QUARTER
2/6   BA 6   Snell for 3 (Gaubatz). Baltimore offsides, loses 3
2/3   BA 3   Snell for no gain (Volk)
3/3   BA 3   Mathis left for 1 (Gaubatz)
4/2   BA 2   J. Turner kicks 9-yard field goal
Score: New York 16 Baltimore 0; Time of drive: 3:58

Johnson kicks off 6-yards deep in end zone. Pearson returns to BA 27
(Richards).
13:10
1/10   BA 27   Unitas to Mackey for 5 (Grantham)
2/5   BA 32   Matte sweeps right for 7 (Baker) 1st down
1/10   BA 39   Unitas to Richardson for 5 (Sample)
2/5   BA 44   Matte left for 19 (Hudson) 1st down
1/10   NY 37   Hill right for 12 (Baird) 1st down
1/10   NY 25   Unitas incomplete to Richardson—overthrown
2/10   NY 25   Unitas pass to Orr intercepted by Beverly in end zone
11:06
1/10   NY 20   Boozer middle on draw for 2 (Miller)
2/8   NY 22   Snell left for 2 (Porter)
3/6   NY 24   Boozer left end on pitch out for 7 (Gaubatz) 1st down
1/10   NY 31   Snell left for 10 (Curtis). Baltimore penalized 15 for

		personal foul. Two 1st downs.
1/10	BA 45	Snell over middle for 7 (Bubba Smith)
2/3	BA 37	Boozer right for 2 (B.R. Smith)
3/1	BA 35	Mathis left for no gain (Michaels)
4/1	BA 35	J. Turner misses 42-yard field goal attempt
6:34		
1/10	BA 20	Unitas incomplete to Mackey (broken up by Grantham)
2/10	BA 20	Unitas incomplete to Richardson—overthrown
3/10	BA 20	Unitas incomplete to Mackey—overthrown
4/10	BA 20	Unitas to Orr for 17 (Beverly) 1st down
1/10	BA 37	Unitas incomplete to Richardson—overthrown
2/10	BA 37	Unitas incomplete short to Hill
3/10	BA 37	Unitas to Mackey for 11 (Baird). New York penalized 15 yards for personal foul. Two 1st downs.
1/10	NY 37	Matte left for 1 (Biggs)
2/9	NY 36	Unitas to Richardson for 21 (Sample) 1st down
1/10	NY 15	Unitas incomplete to Matte—overthrown
2/10	NY 15	Unitas to Orr for 11 (Beverly). New York penalized half the distance for personal foul. Two 1st downs
1/2	NY 2	Matte left for no gain (Rochester). New York penalized half the distance for offsides.
1/1	NY 1	Unitas keeps middle for no gain (Biggs)
2/1	NY 1	Matte right for no gain (Atkinson)
3/1	NY 1	Hill left for the touchdown. Michaels kick PAT

Score: New York 16 Baltimore 7

Michaels boots onside kick, recovered by Baltimore's Mitchell at NY 44

3:14		
1/10	NY 44	Unitas to Richardson for 6 (Sample)
2/4	NY 38	Unitas to Orr for 14 (Beverly) 1st down
1/10	NY 24	Unitas to Richardson for 5
2/5	NY 19	Unitas incomplete to Richardson (broken up by Sample)
3/5	NY 19	Unitas incomplete short to Orr
4/5	NY 19	Unitas incomplete to Orr—overthrown
2:21		
1/10	NY 20	Snell right for 1 (Bubba Smith)
2/9	NY 21	Snell right for 6 (Logan)
3/3	NY 27	Snell right for 4 (Gaubatz) 1st down

1/10	NY 31	(1:54) Snell right for 2 (Boyd)
2/8	NY 33	(1:18) New York loses five yards for delay of game
2/13	NY 28	(1:08) Snell right for 1 (B.R. Smith)
3/12	NY 29	(0:35) New York loses five yards for delay of game
3/17	NY 24	(0:22) Snell sweeps left for 3 (Austin)
4/13	NY 27	(0:15) Johnson punts to BA 34. Brown runs out of bounds.
0:08		
1/10	BA 34	Unitas incomplete to Richardson—overthrown
2/10	BA 34	Unitas to Richardson for 15 (Sample) 1st down

END OF GAME: NEW YORK 16 BALTIMORE 7

1968 New York Jets/Super Bowl III Trivia Quiz

Here's a fun little exercize to test your knowledge of the Jets and the game that changed pro football. Answer 15-25 correctly and you should own a Super Bowl ring. Answer fewer than 15 and you must buy another copy of this book.

1. The week before Super Bowl III, who said, "We better stop watching these films or we'll get overconfident"?
   a. Joe Namath
   b. Don Maynard
   c. Pete Lammons
   d. Johnny Sample
   e. Steve Sabol of NFL Films

2. Name three starters from the 1968 Jets who were once property of the Colts.

3. Which 1968 Jet intercepted two of Namath's passes when Texas beat Alabama in the 1965 Orange Bowl?
   a. Pete Lammons
   b. Jim Hudson
   c. George Sauer
   d. Ralph Baker
   e. Larry Grantham

4. What is Weeb Ewbank's given name?
   a. Wilber
   b. Walt
   c. William
   d. Weebster
   e. Wellington

5. True or False: In the 1968 Super Bowl season, Joe Namath set a then-pro record with 4,007 yards passing.

6. Match these 1968 Jets with their college teams:

a. Dave Herman	a. Buffalo
b. Matt Snell	b. Hofstra
c. Don Maynard	c. Ohio State
d. John Schmitt	d. Michigan State
e. Gerry Philbin	e. Texas Western

7. Name three AFL quarterbacks Joe Namath thought were better than Earl Morrall in 1968.

8. What grooming product did "The Four Jets" sing about in a 1968 television commercial?
   a. Brylcreem
   b. Score Hair Cream
   c. Vitalis
   d. Grecian Formula
   e. Dippity-Do

9. With whom did Joe Namath engage in a celebrated "brawl" before Super Bowl III?
   a. Walt Michaels
   b. Lou Michaels
   c. Bubba Smith
   d. Billy Ray Smith
   e. Howard Cosell

10. Where did Joe Namath make his famous "guarantee" of a Jets Super Bowl III victory?
    a. At a Miami Jai-Lai match
    b. At a Miami restaurant
    c. At a Miami awards dinner
    d. At the pool of the Jets' hotel
    e. In the Colts' lockerroom before the game

11. Which players who were teammates in college went head-to-head on the scrimmage line in Super Bowl III?

12. What was the Super Bowl called before Super Bowl III?
    a. Super Bowl II
    b. The Climax Bowl
    c. The AFL-NFL World Championship Game
    d. The Heidi Bowl
    e. The Pro Football Championship Game

13. What was the name of the trick play the Colts failed to execute at the end of the first half of Super Bowl III?
    a. Flea-flicker
    b. Statue of Liberty
    c. Halfback option
    d. Razzle-dazzle
    e. The improvisation

14. Match these players with their Super Bowl III injuries:
    a. Joe Namath   a. Concussion
    b. Johnny Unitas   b. Thumb
    c. Bubba Smith   c. Shoulder
    d. Al Atkinson   d. Ankle
    e. Rick Volk   e. Elbow

15. What kind of Oakland Raiders turnover secured the Jets' AFL championship game victory in 1968?
    a. a Johnny Sample interception
    b. a blocked punt
    c. an incomplete lateral
    d. a Fred Biletnikoff fumble
    e. a Daryle Lamonica fumble after Verlon Biggs' sack

213

16. Which Jet fumbled the kickoff that was turned into the Oakland Raiders' second touchdown in the last minute of the "Heidi Game"?
    a. John Dockery
    b. Randy Beverly
    c. Earl Christy
    d. Mike Battle
    e. Little Eddie Bell

17. Name the rookie offensive lineman the Jets had to bench, which led to Dave Herman's move from offensive guard to tackle.
    a. Randy Rasmussen
    b. Sam Walton
    c. Joe Walton
    d. Bill Walton
    e. John-Boy Walton

18. Jets punter Curley Johnson put his teammates' impending battle with mighty Baltimore into perspective with the philosophical phrase . . .
    a. "Colts ain't nothin' but another football team."
    b. "Chicken ain't nothin' but a bird."
    c. "Nixon ain't nothin' but a Republican."
    d. "An akita ain't nothin' but a dog."
    e. "Borscht ain't nothin' but beet soup."

19. Which famous figure of the late '60s was reportedly a big Jets fan?
    a. Janis Joplin
    b. Neil Armstrong
    c. Spiro Agnew
    d. Max Yasgur
    e. Abbie Hoffman

20. The major impact of the Jets' Super Bowl III victory on pro football was:
    a. It forced the AFL and NFL to initiate the first merger talks
    b. It finally legitimized the AFL in the minds of the media and the public
    c. It led to widespread use of panty-hose underneath uniform pants on very cold days
    d. If forced Joe Namath to give up his interest in a New York restaurant called "Bachelor's III"
    e. It was directly responsible for ABC-TV launching Howard Cosell and "Monday Night Football"

21. Match these Jets assistant coaches from the '60s with the team they went on to head coach:
    a. Chuck Knox   a. New Jersey Generals
    b. Clive Rush   b. Philadelphia Eagles
    c. Walt Michaels   c. Boston Patriots
    d. Buddy Ryan   d. Buffalo Bills

22. True or False. Don Shula avenged his Super Bowl III defeat by coaching the Colts to a victory in Super Bowl V against the Dallas Cowboys.

23. Which Jets co-owner took over the club as President when Sonny Werblin was bought out prior to the 1968 season?
    a. Leon Hess
    b. Bill Shea
    c. Donald Trump
    d. Phil Iselin
    e. None of the above

24. Who set a Jets club record for sacks in 1968 with 19 and held that record until Mark Gastineau and Joe Klecko broke it in 1981?
    a. John Elliott
    b. Verlon Biggs
    c. Gerry Philbin
    d. Al Atkinson
    e. Larry Grantham

25. Match these sportswriters with the publication they covered the Jets for in 1968:

   a. Paul Zimmerman   a. New York Daily News
   b. Dick Young   b. Sports Illustrated
   c. Dave Anderson   c. New York Post
   d. Tex Maule   d. Bronx Junior High 117 Gazette
   e. Stephen Hanks   e. New York Times

Answers: 1–c. 2–Winston Hill, Johnny Sample, Bill Baird (non-starters were Mark Smolinsky, Curley Johnson, Bake Turner). 3–a. 4–a. 5–False, he set the record in 1967. 6–a-d, b-c, c-e, d-b, e-a. 7–Bob Griese, Dolphins; Daryl Lamonica, Raiders; John Hadl, Chargers; Len Dawson, Chiefs; Babe Parilli, Jets. 8–b. 9–b. 10–c. 11–Dave Herman and Bubba Smith. 12–c. 13–a. 14–a-b, b-e, c-d, d-c, e-a. 15–c. 16–c. 17–b. 18–b. 19–d. 20–b. 21–a-d, b-c, c-a, d-b. 22–False, Shula had become head coach of the Miami Dolphins after the 1969 season. Don McCaffery coached Baltimore in 1970. 23–e (Donald Lillis, who died after the '68 season. Philip Iselin became the new president in '69). 24–c. 25–a-c, b-a, c-e, d-b, e-d.